IF I SURVIVE

Nazi Germany and the Jews
100-year-old Lena Goldstein's
Miracle Story

Faces of Eve Series, No. 1

BARBAR

D1166537

Barbara Miller /Barbara Miller Books
PO Box 425 Westcourt
Cairns, Australia 4870
www.barbara-miller-books.com

Ordering Information:
Quantity sales. Special discounts are available on quantity purchases by corporations, associations, and others. For details, contact the "Special Sales Department" at the address above.

If I Survive: Nazi Germany and the Jews,
100-year-old Lena Goldstein's Miracle Story /Barbara Miller
—1st ed.

Faces of Eve Series no 1

Cover photos - top: Warsaw, Poland, 1943, Waffen SS soldiers beside a burning building during the Warsaw Ghetto Uprising, Yad Vashem Archives, Jerusalem 4613/733

Bottom: German Stormtroopers Force Warsaw Ghetto Dwellers to Evacuate Their Homes, Yad Vashem Photo Archives, Jerusalem 359_76

ISBN 978-0-9953691-9-1 ebook mobi (kindle)
ISBN 978-0-9953691-8-4 paperback
ISBN 978-0-6484722-0-9 eBook EPUB

DOWNLOAD FREE GIFT NOW

Just to thank you for buying my book, I would like to give you a 14-page PDF of the hidden history of the first contact of Europeans with Australian Aborigines. It was at Mapoon. It is the untold story that is not in your school text books. Hear from Aborigines who have had the story passed down through generations and from the explorers.

For information on my other books go to –
www.barbara-miller-books.com

TO DOWNLOAD GO TO
http://eepurl.com/dn69ab

About the Author

This is Barbara's second book on the Holocaust with the first being the biography of William Cooper in 2012. He was an Aboriginal Australian who, as well as being an activist for his people, led a protest against Kristallnacht, the start of the Holocaust or Shoah in 1938. She wrote a historical biography in 2014 on European adventurers who were the first to land on Australian soil in 1606. This was followed in 2018 with her memoir, *White Woman Black Heart* and *The Dying Days of Segregation in Australia*.

This gripping biography of Lena Goldstein is the first in a series called *Faces of Eve* and has come out of Barbara's long history of involvement with the Jewish community in Australia and her 10 trips to Israel with husband Norman attending Christian conferences and leading tour groups. Barbara is a pastor, mediator, psychologist, sociologist. She lives in Cairns, Australia. She was shortlisted in 2018 for the Queensland Literary Awards for a "Work of State Significance" for her memoir.

Reviews

This is a compelling, indeed exemplary work, that merges the history of the Holocaust with the live story of one survivor: Lena Goldstein, aged 100, one of the last living witnesses to the horrors of the Holocaust.

Barbara Miller is helping to keep Lena's voice alive, in doing so, she fulfils the Jewish Mitzvah of Zachor - To Remember:

Konrad Kwiet, Emeritus Professor and Resident Historian Sydney Jewish Museum.

****

Lena Goldstein is perhaps one of the last survivors at the age of 100 who witnessed personally the situation and conditions which existed in the Warsaw ghetto during World War II. The deportations and the rumours of mass killings (at the time thought unbelievable) proved to be true. Lena survived as she said by miracles but if it were not for her positive spirit, resilience and humour the outcome could have been very different. Barbara Miller's work is extremely informative not only of the conditions of that time but also of the historical background that created the opportunity for what we now know as the Holocaust and ultimately the destruction of European Jewry. The world looked away!!!

Eva Engel, OAM, Founder of the first Australian 2nd Generation of the Holocaust Group and first Child Survivor of the Holocaust Group

****

In this concise, compact and highly readable book, the author and her subject have collaborated to produce an invaluable record of not merely one person's extraordinary experiences but of the backdrop of horrific world events. Lena Goldstein found in Barbara Miller the ideal biographer and together they document the real, living, complex human beings who faced, and perpetrated, incredible evil. The reader is quickly drawn in to the world of those whom the Nazis had targeted for murder, with the challenges and complexities facing a single individual given the context of the brutality of some and the kindness of others. Barbara Miller allows each reader to learn and also encourages deep reflection on how humankind could include such an episode in its story.

Lena Goldstein has shaped many lives through telling her personal story of a survival which in many ways appears miraculous, although her interactions were, at every stage, with men and women who themselves were making life and death choices. While her story is unique, it provides a window into a world which never should have been - and now should never be forgotten.

"If I Survive" deserves to be read widely, discussed and, above all, appreciated. The humanity, personal dignity and integrity of Lena Goldstein is inspirational. It is to the author's great credit that she has produced a wonderful, multi-dimensional account of this extraordinary woman's life."

Jeremy Jones AM, former President of the Executive Council of Australian Jewry, Chair, Australian National Dialogue of Christians, Muslims & Jews, Director, Australia/Israel & Jewish Affairs Council

****

How was it possible that some Jews managed to survive the Nazi regime?

This is Lena's riveting personal story of her long years evading the fate of being captured and murdered like so many of her family and friends. It is one of a heroic eye witness and now 100-year-old "memory keeper" to a time and place in history that needs to be remembered not only to validate the fate of those who perished but for the generations who follow.

Barbara Miller's carefully researched book, enriched by Lena's telling of her own story, describes Lena's early days in Lublin, Poland, in the 1920s surrounded by a loving family, close community ties and abundant culture. Germany's calculated invasion of Poland on September 1st 1939 created a world of state sponsored anti-Jewish terror, persecution on the streets, starvation in the ghettos and mass deportations to death camps.

It should not be forgotten. Lena's ultimate survival, like that of other Holocaust survivors, depended on the selfless acts of genuine kindness by strangers who risked their lives and those of their own families to resist the evil injustice of Jewish genocide.

The strong message resonating throughout this powerful book is "to inspire and inform future generations to never lose hope."

Viv Parry, Chairperson, Child Survivors of the Holocaust, Melbourne

****

Another important book from the celebrated writer Barbara Miller. Expertly researched and skillfully written, this personal story of a hundred-year-old Warsaw Ghetto survivor becomes a heart-wrenching narrative of heroism and perseverance against all odds. A significant addition to the Holocaust studies, this book is a must-read.

Irene Shaland, author of *The Dao of Being Jewish and Other Stories: Seeking Jewish narrative all over the World*

****

In Lena Goldstein's story, we journey from her youth in Lublin Poland, through her life and death struggle in the Warsaw Ghetto, to a new life in Australia. Weaving this within the historical context, author Barbara Miller creates a gripping account of how Lena survived the lowest ebb in Jewish history. Lena's story will inspire the next generation to be upstanders, and always to have hope!

Eli Rabinowitz, Educator, genealogist and filmmaker - WE ARE HERE! Foundation

****

Author's note - Hirsh Glik, age 22, wrote the Partisans' Song, *Zog Nit Keynmol*, in the Vilna Ghetto in 1943. Written in Yiddish, it means "Never Say". He was inspired by the Warsaw Ghetto Uprising and the partisan cause generally. It is a powerful song of resistance and has been the hymn of Holocaust survivors for generations. Now, through an international project of the WE ARE HERE! Foundation, the Partisans' Song is inspiring a new generation of Upstanders. It is now being sung in different languages, even in one of the Australian Aboriginal languages – *Noongar*. For more information see the following link:

http://www.jwire.com.au/partisans-song-translated-from-yiddish-to-noongar/

****

By opening the door and allowing us to see into the life of Lena Goldstein, Barbara Miller has actually allowed us to gaze upon a whole generation of Holocaust victims, those that perished at the hands of the Nazis and those that survived.

This book is a tribute to human resilience. Lena Goldstein, like so many others, demonstrated that the human spirit can rise to a point of being unconquerable. We read about the loss of her family, her emotions on the day of her boyfriend's birthday, knowing that he was not spared to see his 27th year and the isolation she felt upon freedom, realising that there was not one person in the whole world waiting for her. In spite of this, Lena triumphs and to this day continues to tell her story, and the story of the Holocaust, so she can play her part to fulfill the dream "Never Again".

We must all learn from this book. The kindness of the caretaker who risked his life to help Lena, and the actions of Lena's father who shared his inadequate food with a desperate old man teach us that every one of us can make a difference.

In this book, Barbara Miller has reinforced this lesson with passion and power through a terrifying account of the atrocities suffered by Lena Goldstein and millions of others during the Holocaust. This book deserves to play a part in shaping human behavior into the future.

John Searle, Barrister, Melbourne, Former Chairperson, Victorian Equal Opportunity and Equal Rights Commission, President of the Jewish Community Council of Victoria and Chairman of the B¹nai B¹rith Anti Defamation Commission.

****

One of my heroes is Nobel Laureate and Holocaust survivor, Elie Wiesel. I quote from his Memoir *A Jew Today*, Chapter "A Plea for the Survivors:"

"The victims were naive enough to feel certain that the so-called civilised world knew nothing of their plight. If the killers could kill freely, it was only because the Allies were not informed.

"If only the Allies knew......people said to one another in the ghettos and in the camps. If only Roosevelt knew. If only Churchill knew. If only the Pope knew. If only they knew.... The victims steadfastly believed that when they knew, the situation would change immediately.

They were wrong, people knew and remained silent. People knew and did nothing. Fortunately, the survivors found out only after the Liberation."

The message that Barbara Miller impresses on us through this interview with Lena Goldstein is to be wary of those who deny the Holocaust, be wary of their evil intent to maybe revisit it. Thank you, Barbara.

I make these comments as child refugee from Nazi Europe (reffo as I was called at school).

Josie Lacey OAM, Author of *An Inevitable Path, A Memoir*, Founder and Convenor Women's Interfaith Network, Convenor NGO Religions For Peace NSW, Life Member Executive Council of Australian Jewry, WIZO, and ECC.

Dedication

I would like to dedicate this book to the God of Abraham, Isaac and Jacob and His Messiah who has given me the inspiration and persistence to write this book. It is also dedicated to Lena as part of her legacy of a life well lived and to her family. I would also like to dedicate this book to my husband Norman, the love of my life who has encouraged and supported me throughout. I also dedicate it to my son Michael and his daughter Jaydah who I love dearly and my wonderful family, the Millers and Russells.

I want to dedicate it also to those who lost their lives in the Holocaust or Shoah and their families; also, to survivors and children of survivors. Let Lena's voice and their voices live on.

Acknowledgements

This book would not have been written without the delightful and gracious Lena, whose story it is and I can't thank her enough for allowing me to tell it. I would like to thank my husband Norman for sacrificing time with me so I could finish this book and for his love and support and the support of family and friends who pray for me. Norman also recorded all my interviews with Lena and Maurice Linker also recorded the first one. Thanks also go to Eva Engel who has been amazingly helpful. When I told her about the Faces of Eve series I wanted to write, she suggested I interview Lena and made the introductions. Eva has been a facilitator of the process all along the way.

I also thank Kerry Davies for professional editing. Thanks as well to Lena and Stanley Goldstein for revisions on the first draft and Emeritus Professor Dr Konrad Kwiet, the Resident Historian at the Sydney Jewish Museum, for helpful comments on the unedited manuscript.

I am grateful to the following people for wonderful reviews – Konrad Kwiet, Eva Engel, Jeremy Jones, Viv Parry, Irene Shaland, Eli Rabinowitz, John Searle and Josie Lacey. Thanks to Aviva Wolff for organising my book launch at the Sydney Jewish Museum and Viv Parry for organising my book launch at the Jewish Holocaust Centre in Melbourne.

Thanks to Yad Vashem for allowing me to use historical photos of the Holocaust. Also, to Rodolfo Samson for the book cover and formatting and to David Jack for help re photographs. Thanks to Paul Green and Ron and Martin Goldstein for the provision of family photographs and Paul for a video. Thanks to Anastasia Uricher for the photo of the bunker model that she put so much time into making.

Foreword

You will not be able to put this book down as it is a fast-paced story of heroism and survival in the midst of the most appalling conditions as Jews and other minorities faced not just religious persecution and racism but the evil Nazi death machine. Lena's compassion and humour stand out in the midst of this horror story. She is an engaging person and shows the human spirit can win through the most horrifying circumstances.

I admire Barbara's tenacity and patience she showed during the research she did to put a context on Lena's story and embed it in the history of the time. I saw the heartbreak Barbara experienced as she wrote this book and poured her heart into it. It is a history we should never forget but we should be saying with the Jewish people *never again*. As an Australian Aboriginal person, I hope you can stand with me and say *never again*.

I was glad to be able to travel with Barbara to Sydney three times in the 2016-2018 period to interview Lena and to do the recording with Barbara's phone and my iPad and I look forward to joining Lena for her 100th birthday on 31 January 2019.

This is a self-published book and it has been self-funded in every aspect from the beginning. I believe this shows Barbara's commitment to the telling of Lena's story. Though there have been a number of newspaper and magazine articles about Lena and even videos, this book enables her story to be told in more detail and it will touch your heart.

Munganbana Norman Miller

Preface

This book was a steep learning curve for me but I appreciate the opportunity to tell such an important story. Lena's story puts a human face on a tragic episode in our history and brings to life a history that we should never forget so we don't repeat it. This book is richly informed by Lena's life and the historical context lets us know what was going on behind the scenes.

Hitler's main target was the Jews who he wanted to wipe off the face of Europe. This reminds me of how some Middle Eastern nations would like to wipe Israel off the map today and drive the Jews into the sea. It is the same genocidal spirit. The focus of this book is on the Holocaust of the Jews.

However, there were other targets of Hitler and Nazism – Poles and other Slavic people, Roma (Gypsies), Catholic priests and Christian pastors, Jehovah's Witnesses, homosexuals, political prisoners and the disabled. Germans married to Jews had to choose between divorce and concentration camps. In all, there were 11 million victims of Hitler's racist diabolical ideology with its blood lust, power lust and greed.

Lena's voice reminds us now, and will inform future generations, what it was like to be a Jew during the Holocaust. Some voices were silenced by gunshots, bayonet stabbings, the gas chambers or a burning ghetto. Other voices were silenced by torturous living conditions in the ghetto, where starvation, disease and psychological warfare were rife.

But the voices of men and women who wrote diaries or who recorded their stories by video or audio will continue to speak to future generations long after they have left this earth. Their testimony helps us to believe these unbelievable horrors actually occurred, despite Holocaust deniers who will not face these uncomfortable facts.

For those who survived and those who didn't survive – their voices still speak and echo down the decades.

> And the LORD said, "What have you done? The voice of your brother's blood is crying to me from the ground."
>
> —Genesis 4:10

This is a cry for justice.

****

FACES OF EVE SERIES

This is the first book in the Faces of Eve Series. The series is about Jewish women from Europe and the Middle East and Middle Eastern women who live in Sydney, Australia, and their experiences of having to leave desperate situations in their nations and migrate to Australia.

Contents

A Holocaust Survivor

I don't want the Holocaust to be forgotten, because it should serve as a lesson for future generations.

–Lena Goldstein

Hiding from the Nazis with other Jews in a makeshift bunker in Warsaw as World War Two raged, the beautiful young woman with big brown eyes and light brown hair reached for her diary. She had secreted it in a crevice with a few precious photos and her passport, her only possessions. She looked around her cave-like hideout in the subterranean water channels under the city.

The roof was so low she couldn't stand and walk but she shuffled herself into a sitting position to write. Her stomach was rumbling from lack of food and she yearned to wash and change her clothes. But they couldn't foul their drinking water and she'd had only the clothes on her back all these months. She tried not to let the lice distract her. "Will I survive?" she asked herself. "Or will the Germans discover and kill us?" She longed for a normal life. It was November 1944 and the young woman was Helena Midler:

> I long for the splatter of autumn rain. I long
> for the monotonous music of raindrops beating
> with fine drizzle against a window pane; for the
> grey, melancholy, clouded November sky. And I

> long for the thoughts; thoughts at a twilight hour,
> the thoughts which, sad as they might be, never
> begin with the words, "If I survive…", and never
> carry the burden of doubt that all this thinking is
> empty and pointless, because… I will not survive
> anyway. Outside the rain is falling.

Outside, the rain was falling, but, inside, Lena's tears did not fall. She had hidden them away as surely as she had hidden herself away. It wasn't safe to come out into the open and it wasn't safe to cry. What would she unleash if she did? And could she bear it?

"If I survive!" The thought kept coming. She could not erase it. There was no certainty. Death was all around her. She had to keep the will to survive beating in her heart. She could not give up, give in, to despair. She had to carry on, one seemingly endless day after the next, wondering when the war would end. When would it all be over? And who would care if she survived?

Lena Goldstein (nee Midler) didn't expect to make it to her one hundredth birthday. Her story is a miracle of survival from the Shoah, better known as the Holocaust. She could have been one of the three million Polish Jews killed by the Nazi machine. But she was one of the 10 per cent who survived.

Lena recalled the last words her older brother said to her: "Somebody has to survive to tell the world what happened because it is unbelievable." The Germans killed him in the Warsaw Ghetto Uprising, and she narrowly missed this fate herself. They could have killed Lena in the death camp of Treblinka like other family members, but she escaped such a tragic end. However, she led a terrible, dehumanising existence in the ghetto and later in hiding like a hunted creature.

Lena shakes her head and looks at me with eyes widening: "It was unbelievable." For a long time, she couldn't tell her story. The enormity of it and the ache in her heart pulled back the words before they were on her lips. Could she relive the pain? Would she be retraumatised each time she told her story? But one day she knew she had to fulfil her brother's request and speak for those, like him, who could not speak for themselves – for their lives were cruelly torn from them.

Lena's diminutive figure belies her towering personality. She is gracious and cheerful. Her memory and energy are amazing. Perfectly coiffured, tinted blond hair frames her lined face, and she always dresses in an elegant style. She moves around easily as if there are no aches and pains to go with her age. I looked around her room the first day I interviewed her, in 2016, seeing shelves of photos of her family born since her arrival in Australia as a refugee, now seventy years ago. She was living on her own then, a widow, and, despite her ninety-seven years was feisty and sprightly. Her home was cosy and inviting. Family members dropped in to check on her while we talked.

Eva Engel and her friend Maurice Linker had driven my husband Norman and me to Lena's Dover Heights Sydney home for the interview. Eva is a mover and shaker in the Sydney Jewish community and voluntarily makes presentations on the Holocaust for the Sydney Jewish Museum and the organisation Courage to Care. Her enthusiasm for community projects never falters. I first met her when I launched my book about Holocaust protestor William Cooper, an Aboriginal activist of the early 1900s, at the museum in 2012.

Eva likes to connect people. She introduced me to Kayla Szumer, who was then living on the Sunshine Coast. Norman and I visited Kayla and she showed us a video of the work of Courage to Care. I was so impressed, I persuaded the Catholic Church in Cairns to introduce the anti-bullying program to their many schools in north Queensland where I live. Kayla and Maurice were part of the team who came to Cairns in 2015.

When I asked her if I could interview her for my Faces of Eve book series, she agreed but said, "You must interview Lena. She has an amazing story and has just been telling it to schoolchildren in Poland by Skype."

I agreed and Lena's is an eye-opening story. Eva has her straight grey hair swept up, and she brightens up the conversation with her smiles and colourful clothes. She has her own story and works with

3

children of survivors. Maurice, a quiet supporter with grey hair and wrinkles revealing his years, has his own account of Shoah survival. Eva took charge of our first interview as she knew Lena's story so well. Maurice and Norman recorded it.

Australia is a place of refuge for more Holocaust survivors per capita than anywhere else in the world except for Israel. In the first couple of years after World War Two, about 27,000 Jewish refugees made their home in Australia. Of the 7000 left, 3000 live in Sydney.

Lena's horror story seems incongruent with the comfortable, safe surroundings of her home but she tells it without self-pity, without bitterness and without an attempt to shock the listener. It is her passion to tell her story so the generations that follow will maintain a vigilance to ensure the atrocities of the Holocaust will never happen again, not just to Jews but to any vulnerable group.

Aged in her late nineties, Lena still lectures for school students, university students and anyone else who will listen. There are no signs that she plans on stopping. Thankyou letters from schoolchildren who have heard her remarkable story overflow her drawers. Like the thankyou letters that tumble out, Lena's words calmly tumble out, building a picture of a world gone crazy, spinning off its axis, upended and in chaos.

So where does her story start? Lena was born Helena Midler to a comfortable, cultured, middle-class family in Lublin, Poland. Her father's name was Usher, and her mother's name was Gitle. Her brothers Mathis and Israel (more commonly called Salek) were born in 1910 and 1913. Lena's sister Fela, similar to the name Felicity, was born in 1912. Lena was the youngest of the four siblings, born soon after the end of World War One, on 31 January 1919.

As a four-year-old, her big brown eyes looked up at the camera, not smiling, as if she was not sure of what was happening. The large bow on top of her head, and the cute outfit reminiscent of post-World War One Poland, signifies how adored she was by her parents. It was the only photo of herself she managed to save through the trials and persecution to come.

Lena has only one photo of her father and mother, preciously held onto through perilous times and greatly cherished. Her father looks pensive, his brown eyes seemingly looking into a future that was elusive. Yet he has the air of someone who was determined to make the best of things. Bald, with thick eyebrows, he always dressed well. This seems to have set the trend for the family. Gitle's blond hair was tied back, as is Fela's as they are pictured enjoying an outing on a cold winter's day. Mathis and Salek have dark hair and, as Lena said, are good looking. Mathis' eyes are obscured because of the quality of the photo but Salek's eyes look piercingly at the viewer.

Lena's father was a partner in a private bank, until the bank went out of business, and was well respected. He belonged to a club of the intelligentsia in Lublin, where usually only people with "good education" could belong, even though her father was not well educated. Lena said, "There were five Jews at the Intelligentsia Club with no tertiary education. If Jews disagreed with each other, certainly in civil matters, they would seek justice through a Jewish "court", and there was no appeal. Learned and wise men, such as the rabbi, formed a panel of judges, and among them was my father in an honorary capacity."

The Midlers was a *kosher* household, but not overtly religious. Lena went to a Polish school and said she didn't feel anti-Semitism there. Even so, on reflection she recalls that while she was able to play with the non-Jewish children, she wasn't allowed to visit their homes. She said:

> I went to a Polish school and was friends with everybody, and they came to my place. My brothers were nice boys, good looking, with a good sense of humour. My sister's friends and my friends came often. I was never invited to my friends' homes. I don't know what my friends' houses looked like. They would do their homework at my place.

I was the youngest of my year at a girls'
school. In the higher classes, everyone had a boyfriend. I was very small, compared with the other
girls, as well as being young, so I had no boyfriend,
and I often served as a chaperone. I followed the
couple and had to watch them. So, I had to read
to pass the time.

The family put great store on education, so Lena looked forward to
becoming a lawyer. Intelligent and well read, she dreamed of changing
the world for the better and had a desire to help others. Lena was a
bright and friendly young woman with a ready smile. A smart dresser,
slim, poised and graceful, she had a wonderful life ahead of her. Or
so it seemed. But, with the rise of Hitler and the Nazis in nearby
Germany, the world, and her own life, were to change dramatically.

1. Eva Engel, Lena Goldstein and Barbara Miller
at Lena's Sydney home Jan 2016

2. Lena Midler, 4 years old

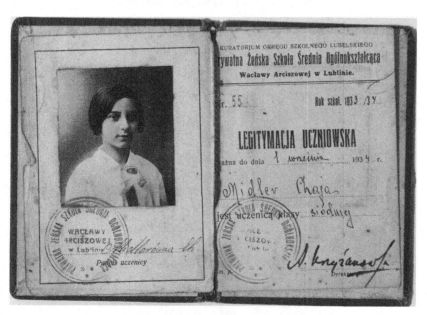

3. Helena (Chaja) Midler as a schoolgirl

4. Usher Midler, Lena's father

5. Gitle and Mathis Midler, Lena's mother and brother

6. Mathis Midler

7. Fela and Gitle Midler, Lena's sister and mother

8. Salek, Lena's brother

9. Lena Midler

2

Poland

This meant they knew exactly who was Jewish and who was not [at Warsaw University]. So, in the intervals, they used to beat us up. They didn't just smack us. They beat us up so that some of us were finishing up in the hospital.

—Lena Goldstein

Poland is at the centre of this story, not only Lena's birthplace. Poland had the largest Jewish population in all of Europe. It suffered the highest number of Jewish casualties of the Holocaust, about three million Jews perishing. A report by the government of Poland in 1947 estimated the Nazi death machine killed the same number of non-Jewish Poles, but later estimates have it at about 1.9 million, which is still very significant (United States Holocaust Memorial Museum 2018b). Nearly 1.5 million Polish citizens were sent to Germany and camps for slave labour. Hitler's onslaught was meant to strike terror into the Poles, with the leaders and intelligentsia struck down first.

Poland was the only nation for which Hitler issued a decree that all Poles hiding Jews would be killed on the spot, and all their family with them, even children. Many Polish families were martyred for helping Jews, and many of them were Christian. Others became bystanders, either indifferent to the suffering of Jews or too frightened to help. The Yad Vashem World Holocaust Remembrance Center in Jerusalem recognises those who weren't Jewish but who helped save Jews, endangering their own lives as a consequence. Poland has the highest number of these people remembered as the "Righteous Among the Nations". There were also Poles who collaborated with the Nazis, who killed Jews or who were complicit in their deaths.

Unlike most European countries occupied by Nazi Germany, in occupied Poland there was no official collaboration either at the political or economic level, and the Polish government-in-exile operated from France and later Britain. Poland never officially surrendered to the Germans, with the Polish army continuing to fight underground as *Armia Krajowa* and forest partisans – *Leśni*. The Polish resistance movement during World War Two was the largest resistance movement in all of occupied Europe. The Warsaw Ghetto was the largest ghetto in Nazi-occupied Europe, and most of the German concentration camps were in Poland. There has been controversy recently, with the Polish government making it unlawful to describe them as "Polish death camps" because, although the death camps were all in Poland, the German occupation operated them.

The invasion of Poland by Germany was the final straw that led to World War Two.

****

Today, Lublin is the ninth largest city in Poland, with about 350,000 people. For some centuries, Lublin was home to a thriving Jewish community with a widely respected *yeshiva* known as "the Jewish Oxford". It was a centre of learning of *Talmud* and *Kabbalah*. Jews were a vital part of the city's life and, in the historical district, the Grodzka Gate was dubbed the Jewish Gate. They had a synagogue, a Jewish hospital and a Jewish cemetery. The cold, damp winters and warm summers did not dampen people's spirits enough to hinder them from enjoying theatres, museums, art galleries and restaurants. The cobbled streets and historical architecture of the Renaissance city gave it a unique ambience.

Lena's memories of Lublin were of living what she termed "a normal life with a loving family". She was proud of her family and other people talked about them with high esteem. Her brothers and sister would go to the pictures to see a matinee, for instance, and her mother would insist they had to take Lena, the smallest, with them. For Lena, this meant she had an active social life, not only with her own friends but with those of her siblings.

****

However, disaster struck the successful Jewish bank that Lena's father and his partner operated. It was a Jewish bank with mostly Jewish clients – small businessmen. They financed a Polish farmers bank that went bankrupt. Being a man of principles, responsibility and compassion, Usher couldn't live with the thought that the Jews who had put money into his bank would lose it. His partner felt the same way, so he and his partner sold their houses and almost everything they owned, even the chandeliers, to repay their Jewish clients as best they could and prevent them losing their savings. This left Usher and his family bereft of everything, leaving him feeling somewhat belittled, fallen from grace. He moved to Warsaw to look for an alternative living. He still had a good name with Jewish banks and was offered the role of representing one at the stock exchange. Lena remembers:

> My mother was a typical Jewish mother, did everything at home, never complained. The only time I saw her crying was after my father lost the money. Mum went with me to a cousin to borrow money for my schooling. He said, "No, let her do a manual job." She cried on the staircase afterward.
>
> When I was little, my mother and her friends had a club where they helped poor children in Poland. We children did the same, collected our pennies (*grosze*) and gave them to the ladies. We

13

had a big flat, decorated with furniture from a restaurant. Mother would sublet, rent rooms out.

Lena stayed in Lublin after her parents went to Warsaw. She lived with her aunty and, although she was grateful, she was disappointed she couldn't afford a stamp to write to her mother. Lena didn't go to a Jewish school and felt lucky the principal was kind to her. He phoned Lena's mother and offered her a significant discount on school fees and said he'd give Lena a job because her mother couldn't support her. Lena coached three young students. Her payment was being provided breakfast, lunch and dinner, rather than cash.

In time, after completing school, Lena was accepted into Warsaw University and enrolled in law. She couldn't have gone to Lublin University because it was Catholic and they didn't take Jews. Warsaw University accepted some Jews but maintained quotas, and would only allow the same percentage of Jews as in the general population. Her future boyfriend, Simon Rosenkranz, was at the university.

Poland was considered by many as the largest and most important centre of Jewish culture in the world. Most accounts trace the beginning of Jewish settlement in Poland to the fourteenth century, but the Museum of the History of the Polish Jews records their arrival after escaping eleventh-century *pogroms* in western Europe.

"According to Jewish legend, the refugees heard a voice from heaven say 'Po lin', or 'rest here' in Hebrew – and Poland was given its name. 'For centuries, Poland hosted the world's largest Jewish Diaspora,' museum director Andrzej Cudak said. While Jewish culture flourished, religious tolerance had its limits." (World Jewish Congress 2018)

In 1483, Jews were expelled from Warsaw and could only live on the outskirts of the city, not being officially allowed to live in Warsaw proper again until 1768. Jewish businesses, prayer meetings, and charitable associations were set up, and Jewish leaders began to run services and establish traditional Jewish life.

However, organised street fights against the Jews took place after the first partition of Poland, in 1772. In 1775, many Jews were expelled from Warsaw. Russian troops massacred the Warsaw Jews because they took part in the Polish uprising against the Russians during the partition period.

Warsaw became part of Prussia in 1796 and Jews were subject to *Juden Reglements*, which only allowed Jews living in Warsaw before 1796 to stay in the city. In 1805, there was another outbreak of attacks on the Jews by Poles.

In 1809, the Jews established a Jewish quarter in Warsaw. Jewish businessmen, manufacturers, army suppliers and doctors were allowed to live there, on the provision they wore European-style clothing and sent their children to general schools. The Jewish Virtual Library records:

> The population of Warsaw continued to grow in the 19th and 20th century. In 1816, Jews numbered 15,600 and, by 1910, the community reached 337,000 (38% of the total population of Warsaw). This rise was due to mass migration in the 1860s and another set of migrations after the 1881 *pogroms* in Russia, after which 150,000 Jews moved to Warsaw. Many Jews came from Lithuania, Belorussia, and Ukraine. (Jewish Virtual Library 2018d)

Most of Warsaw's synagogues were small, private and located in the backyards of tenements. The Great Synagogue in Tlomackie Square was the largest and most beautiful synagogue in Warsaw and was the only place offering a Reform service. It was frequented by the educated and wealthy. In 1936, the Main Judaic Library was built next to it. The *Bund*, Jewish socialists, was a popular movement among Jewish workers. While they promoted *Yiddish* culture, they were opposed to Zionism and the revival of Hebrew.

Agudat Yisra'el (Union of Israel) was a political movement of Orthodox Jewry, founded at a conference in Kattowitz, now Poland, in May 1912. It spread throughout Europe, the United States and pre-state Israel. Despite the *Bund* receiving the most votes to represent the Jewish community in the Warsaw municipality, the Polish government ignored the 1936 election results, and chose who they wanted. This board was in place until the German occupation.

By 1939, Warsaw had about 380,000 Jews, the second-largest Jewish population in the world after New York City, and about the same number as the whole of France. Jews comprised one-third of the total population of Warsaw (Intrepid Berkley Explorer 2018). Young children played on their tricycles in their gardens; older children were seen in bathing togs while holidaying in a resort town nearby and worship at the synagogue was well attended. Workers were busy in their jobs, including doctors and nurses at the Jewish hospital, and the streets buzzed with life, people shopping and meeting friends at cafés in a typical cosmopolitan lifestyle. Jewish organisations put out 30 daily newspapers and over 130 periodicals, employing about 1000 Jewish workers printing them. The Main Judaic Library and the Institute of Judaic Studies flourished.

Survivor Joel Avigan remembers his childhood in the Jewish Quarter of Warsaw pre-World War Two:

> A poor Jewish widow would come up to our house selling tea and sugar. An elderly Chassidic man would supply us with toilet paper and kitchen soap. Raw milk was brought daily from the neighborhood cowshed, measured and directly poured into the pot for immediate boiling. Each visitor would be occasionally invited to sit down over a cup of tea and a piece of cake and be given the opportunity to tell his story and to pour out his heart. People had somehow a lot of time for each other. (Avigan 2018)

****

Lena looks back down the years, her lined face betraying little of the trauma, mainly the passing of time. She seems to overlook the early anti-Semitism she faced with her Gentile school friends not inviting her to their homes and her not being able to go to Lublin University because of being a Jew. Maybe it pales in significance compared with what Lena faced later. She said: "The first time I felt anti-Semitism is when I moved to Warsaw and I started studying law. The first semester passed quietly. At the beginning of the second semester we got an announcement - everybody had to return their IDs to the office. The ID contained my name, birthdate, religion and the faculty in which I was studying. When they returned the IDs to the office, they had stamped them, all of them. All the Jewish ones had the letter L stamped on them."

Lena frowned, still trying to digest this early sign of segregation, but worse was to come.

> L meant left side, and it meant that all Jewish students had to sit on the left side of the auditorium while all the others had the letter P, which in Polish means right, and so were sitting on the right side of the auditorium.
>
> It made us second-class citizens, so we would refuse to sit there. But we were not allowed to sit with the others, so instead, we chose to stand at the back of the auditorium. This meant they knew exactly who was Jewish and who was not. So, in the intervals, they used to beat us up. They didn't just smack us. They beat us up so that some of us were finishing up in the hospital.

It left not just physical scars but mental and emotional scars. They were made outcasts, unwanted, reviled, even hated. Why? These had been their classmates they had happily sat among, smiled at and talked to in breaks.

Had the Polish students been ordered to act like this; told that Jews might take their jobs when they graduated? Or were there a few student leaders who saw the marginalisation of the Jews and took advantage of it, others mindlessly following? Did others stand by letting it happen, giving it tacit consent, or were some too scared to challenge the behaviour?

Lena reflected: "It was dangerous to go to the lectures. Law is such a faculty that you can study from books. You don't have to listen to the lectures. So, we studied at home from the books until the time of the exams came, but then they refused to let us pass a certain subject because we were not present at the lectures. Every professor signed our IDs that we attended these lectures, except one, and because of this one we were refused to be admitted to the test, and we lost a year. And there was no use repeating the year because the next year would be the same."

Lena's brothers and their friends had to finish studying abroad because they weren't allowed to study in Polish universities. "First, they started in France, and then they moved to Italy because Italy had cheaper education, and they finished medicine in Italy. They came back already able to practise, but they couldn't get registered as doctors in Poland because they were Jewish. The authorities didn't say it was because they were Jewish, but because they had a certificate from abroad," said Lena.

Hitler was already in power in Germany, and Lena thought the Polish government admired what he was doing in Germany.

> We had beautiful woods, wild woods, in Poland, and every year they used to invite the representatives of the German government to take part in the hunting that went on there. Some Poles at that time rather approved of what Hitler was doing. We didn't know about the pact that Germany had with Russia until they attacked Poland.

Anyone can be nasty, but what happened was that, when we arrived, appeared alive after the war, liberated, some Poles would greet us with, "Oh, Hitler didn't finish you off? Shame."

Her voice falters, and she clears her throat. The deep disappointment that some of her countrymen wished her and her family dead lingers on.

10. Jewish Quarter Lublin, Mahararshal Synagogue 1938

11. Warsaw Old City

12. Simon Rosenkranz, Lena's boyfriend

13. Simon Rosenkranz (also called Shimek or Szymek) with Lena and Antek

21

Nazis at War in Europe

We defended a whole month, while countries were falling within days. Countries like France, like Belgium, like Holland, like other countries and Warsaw defended itself.

—Lena Goldstein

The clouds of war hung over Europe like a shroud that was ready to wrap itself around the dead. After coming to power in Germany, Adolf Hitler signed a nonaggression pact with Poland in January 1934 because he was concerned the French and the Poles might make a military alliance against Germany before Germany had a chance to rearm. In the mid and late 1930s, France and especially Britain followed a foreign policy of appeasement. Neither of them in 1938 was militarily prepared to fight a war against Nazi Germany. In attempting to keep the peace:

> Britain and France acquiesced to Germany's rearmament (1935–1937), remilitarization of the Rhineland (1936), and annexation of Austria (March 1938). In September 1938, after signing away the Czech border regions, known as the Sudetenland, to Germany at the Munich conference, British and French leaders pressured France's ally, Czechoslovakia, to yield to

> Germany's demand for the incorporation of those
> regions. (United States Holocaust Memorial
> Museum 2018a)

The Germans sliced up Czechoslovakia in March 1939 in violation of the Munich agreement despite Anglo–French assurances to protect what was left of it. Poland must have wondered how worthwhile were British and French guarantees of its integrity. Hitler then shrewdly negotiated a nonaggression pact with the Soviet Union. The Molotov–Ribbentrop Pact of August 1939, which stated that Poland was to be carved up between the two powers, meant that Germany could attack Poland without the Soviets intervening.

When Nazi Germany invaded Poland, Britain and France decided they could no longer appease Germany. Things were at breaking point. They declared war. It became World War Two.

Lena raises her hands as if to make a point and seems proud of the Polish defence. "We defended a whole month, while countries were falling within days. Countries like France, like Belgium, like Holland, like other countries, and Warsaw defended itself. We didn't have a television set. There were only radios. There was an order coming through the radio, the president of the city of Warsaw, that all able-bodied men had to leave Warsaw and go to the east, and there to join the Polish army."

The Germans were bombing Warsaw. Lena and other young people who hadn't been required to go to the east started digging trenches. Lena remembers the fear and confusion:

> No bomb shelters, people running to cellars. No fridges. Trying to find some way not to be killed, so we dug trenches. It was for nothing. Warsaw defended itself for a whole month but there was no delivery of fresh food. German tanks were fighting against Polish cavalry. People were cutting pieces of furniture for fuel and standing in queues with utensils to get soup from soup kitch-

ens. Tanks and airplanes against horses. How can you fight like this? A lot of Polish Jews lived in Germany and were very patriotic Germans, but Germany forced them return to Poland. Many still said, "When Hitler wins the war, we'll go back."

Germany's strategy was one of *Blitzkrieg* – swift, devastating and inflicting maximum fear. For example, Germany invaded Holland on 10 May 1940, and Holland surrendered six days later. Massive damage had been inflicted on Rotterdam by bombing, and concerns were raised whether Amsterdam could survive such an onslaught.

"When my brothers heard that [the President of Warsaw's announcement], they left Warsaw, and they had to leave hurriedly and as they stood. At that time there was no official clothing for them. Men were wearing their suit, a shirt and a tie. That's how they left to go fight a war."

Lena's brothers did not realise that in the east they would join the Russians. "The Russians…you know, now when I think about it, at the third or fourth day of the war, they ordered us to go east and join the army there. Everybody was fighting. Everybody took part. I was digging the trenches."

So, my brother and others, they were working in a Jewish hospital, as doctors, but without the right of a doctor. They were not registered as doctors. When the war started, the first thing, they went to the office of the army and willingly and voluntarily applied to go into the Polish army as doctors; they would have to accept them as doctors. They went to apply, and you know what the response was? They can't. They can't give them the right to wear…they haven't got enough uniforms for the so-called doctors.

But the east had already been taken by the Russians. There was no Polish army any more to join. Brześć (Brest) was under Russian occupation. Lena recalls it, "Not being required by the Polish army, they went east as all fit Poles had been required to do. When they went east, instead of the Polish army, they met the Russians, but the Russians needed doctors and, although not straight away, after a while, without any rights, my brother became a chief doctor of the hospital in Brest. He took with him about thirty friends. Also, I had my maternal and paternal family living in Brest, so they took care of the asylum seekers, so to say."

Lena has told her heartbreaking story before. Many times. She looks down at the family photo album and closes it – as if to put a space between her and the memories. "He was a doctor with the Russians, and then the Germans attacked Russia, and attacked the city of Brest, and took all of my uncles, and they left the women. They didn't know what happened to my uncles. I was going to take some clothing for my brothers and some of the boys there. They all went as they stood."

To offer what support she could, Lena went undercover as an actress with a troop of actors who happened to be going to Brest.

> We were already on the Russian side, and people were coming back from the Russian side, saying, "Go back, go back because they're killing people," especially Jews, because they know the Jews are escaping from the Germans. They're killing Jews because they know that everybody is selling all that they possess to run away from the Germans to the Russian side. It was dangerous. We had to come back. Even so, when we came back, they decided that somebody has to go. They can't live there forever in one piece of clothing. My sister's husband – new husband – was there in Brest so my parents decided that she

should go to him, and my father paid the smuggler to take them, and she went to Brest.

She couldn't find him. No one seemed to know where he was. Frantically, she searched for her husband. There were no cars, and the trains were going just sporadically. She heard that he had gone to Russia so she determined that she would go from one station to another after another and enquire if anybody had seen somebody who looked like him. She went from one station to another, different cities and towns and how many stops?

Eventually at one station, she got off the train and was standing on one platform asking anyone she could whether they might have seen her husband and somebody came over to her and asked, "What are you doing here?"

She said, "I am looking for my husband."

"What do you mean you're looking for your husband? He's standing there on the other platform going in the opposite direction."

He was heading back to Brest. Miraculously she had found him. Lena counts this as one of many miracles that contributed to her survival and wellbeing.

Lena's sister Fela and her husband did not want to accept Russian citizenship. They were Polish citizens, and they wanted to go back to Poland. Angered, the Russians sent them to Siberia instead, as punishment. Russia had already been sent many dissidents to this remote place. Lena longed to find her sister, hold her in her arms, share sisterly stories, even to know she was alive and not suffering. But there was no word from her. It was as if a chapter of her life had closed.

Meanwhile, the younger of Lena's brothers smuggled himself back to Warsaw and then worked in a basket factory. Her older brother Mathis married amid all the turmoil and had a two-day-old baby daughter. Desperate for their newborn baby to survive, they paid a Polish smuggler to get them onto the Aryan side, the non-Jewish side, to safety.

"However," said Lena, shifting in her chair uncomfortably, "he took them on the Aryan side; he took them to the forest, and he killed them and took their belongings. He killed the three of them."

Her voice trails off. The mother's name was Bronka, but Lena was never to find out the name of the baby. Lena only found out about their deaths later, by accident, as she was always asking questions of people who had come from concentration camps, trying to put the pieces together of what happened to families.

4

Poland Defeated and Warsaw Ghetto Set Up

Children of our neighbours, children we used to play with, they didn't know any German at all except one word only, Jude, and that meant Jew. They were running down between those queues, pointing out Jude, and Jews were expelled from the (soup) queues because Jews don't have to eat That was the first sign of the persecution.

—Lena Goldstein

The Nazis fought their way into Warsaw. Dead bodies were everywhere. They closed the schools, shut down the newspapers and concerts. The people loved music, but the city fell silent.

The Siege of Warsaw by the Germans began on 1 September 1939, one week after the signing of the Molotov–Ribbentrop Pact, while the Soviet invasion of Poland commenced on 17 September. The Polish Warsaw Army (*Armia Warszawa*) defended Warsaw, the capital of Poland, as substantial aerial bombardments by the Luftwaffe rained down.

As Polish radio announced the invasion, the Polish authorities ordered a blackout in preparation for the air raids. The Poles were afraid that, if their apartment took a direct hit, they would be buried alive, so they didn't want to go to their bomb shelters in the first days of

German bombing. But staying in their apartments was not an option either, as they would be exposed to flying glass and shrapnel. Where could they go? So, they huddled in the stairwells and brought with them anything they thought they would need during the air raids, which could last for many hours each day. Before long, they were eating and sleeping there in the stairwells.

At first, families only returned to their apartments at night. As the bombing got heavier and night air raids started, they were ordered to go to their basement bomb shelters. As well as taking water, clothes and bedding, they took barrels of sand to extinguish possible fires. There was no fresh air. The Poles heard the terrifying sounds of the air raids and worried if their apartment would be the next to receive a direct hit. Their sweating, smoking and coughing contaminated the air as they huddled in their shelters.

Holocaust survivor Artur Ney remembers the frightening sound of the nail-studded boots of the German soldiers striding the cobble-stoned streets of Warsaw. He says:

> The Germans soon began shedding their masks, and signs saying *Nur für Deutsche* (For Germans Only) began appearing in the city. Some streets were completely evacuated and occupied by Germans. Then the raids and round-ups began, paralyzing food deliveries, causing price increases and spreading panic throughout Warsaw. In the beginning, the whole population was targeted, and a curfew was imposed on both Poles and Jews. However, the Nazis soon began to target only Jews with taxes, evictions, and expropriations. We were inundated with degrading and panic-inducing orders. (Mackay 2016)

Lena remembers the day. "We were surrounded, and the Germans entered Warsaw. There had been no delivery of fresh food to Warsaw, and the Germans straight away started a soup kitchen for the population. People were standing in queues with their bowls to get some soup. Little boys, they thought it was fun; it was a game. Children of our neighbours, children we used to play with, they didn't know any German at all except one word only, *Jude* and that meant Jew. They were running down between those queues, pointing out *Jude*, and Jews were expelled from the queues because Jews don't have to eat," she said wryly. "That was the first sign of the persecution."

Lena describes the deliberate measures not only to starve the Jewish people into submission but to humiliate them, to try to grind them into the ground, to dehumanise them in the eyes of others and themselves. It required great resilience of the Jewish people to withstand this and to value their humanity and that of others.

> There were things to kill our dignity, like an armband with a Jewish star on it we had to wear. This was different from the yellow star. It meant the same thing, but in Poland you had the armband.
>
> Then men, at that time, all men were wearing hats. The men who pass by a German soldier would have to come down from the pavement onto the road, not to touch the German soldier, and take off their hats and bow. It hurt me when I looked at a person like my father, a respected member of the community, having to bow to this youngster, because he was wearing a German uniform.
>
> That was not all. They would "catch" – we called it "catching". They would catch an elderly Jew with a beard, cut off his beard, and order him to dance in the middle of the street. All the neighbours, all the passersby, standing there laughing. They thought it was so funny. It wasn't funny for us. They'll catch a young girl, ten, eleven, twelve, thirteen years old, order her

to take off her panties and wash the pavement with the panties. Again, that was so funny for them. It wasn't funny for us.

****

Lena was living in an area where there were a lot of Jews. On 2 October 1940, Ludwig Fischer, governor of the Warsaw District in German-occupied Poland, signed the order to officially create the Warsaw Ghetto, the largest ghetto in Nazi-occupied Europe.

An ultimatum was given to all Jewish people in Warsaw to relocate to the ghetto by 15 November 1940, when it was sealed off, initially with barbed wire and later with brick. About 113,000 Gentile Poles were forced to resettle to the 'Aryan side' and were replaced by Jews from other parts of Warsaw. About 4000 Jews from Germany also were deported to the Warsaw Ghetto, which numbered around 450,000 inhabitants, 85,000 of them children under fourteen. With 146,000 people per square kilometre, conditions were very crowded. This meant eight to ten people per room with many being homeless. (Gasior 2018)

Other ghettos were established in Nazi-occupied territory as well. It was a means of controlling, persecuting and breaking the spirit of the Jews until they could decide how to eliminate them entirely. It was a form of segregation, and many Jews died of starvation and disease, their swollen bodies lying on the streets awaiting an unceremonious removal. Grieving families could only cover them with newspaper and recite the *Kaddish*.

Photos and film show the deportation of Jews to the ghetto. As well as adults, there were long lines of children walking, each carrying a chair and wagons loaded with whatever household furniture and goods families could fit on them. Some were pulled by people and some by a horse. Strained faces, bewildered looks, Germans standing by with guns pointed. This exodus from freedom, this exodus from normality, this exodus from all that had constituted their lives, continued for weeks. They left their homes and most of their belongings behind. They left their jobs and means of income. They left friend-ships and hobbies and outings behind. But they still had their dignity and faith, whether that faith was in God or in the will of the Jewish people to survive centuries of persecution.

The Germans surrounded the ghetto with a wall and posted guards on it to prevent people coming and going. Lena's house be-came part of the ghetto, so her family didn't have to move. But every family was allowed one room only, whether there were two people in the family or ten. So Lena's family had to move into only one room in their home and allow two other families to move into their two other rooms. It was very crowded and put pressure on all the facilities, including the toilet. Her brothers had already gone.

Lena recounts the horror of the Warsaw Ghetto, at times her voice dropping: "The order came that all Jews, whether living in this area or the suburbs, or the villages or townships around Warsaw, will have to move to Warsaw and squash into one small area, with 450,000 people. In a way, we were, I wouldn't say happy, but content at least that we won't have direct contact with the Germans, and won't be treated like that. Yeah. Little did we know what was coming. As there is one room per family. It was so overcrowded that people were mostly in the streets."

Many were forced to live on the streets with no protection from the freezing winter, no way of cooking food if they were able to get it somehow, and no place to wash and toilet. The Germans shot those who complained about their treatment or tried to protect others. Some children had no shoes in the freezing winter, and some adults used newspapers to cover their feet. Little children who tried to find a way out of the ghetto to steal or beg for food to smuggle into their family in the ghetto were shot if discovered. There was no mercy. The Nazi propaganda machine had painted Jews as subhuman and a danger to Aryan purity and supremacy. Outside the ghetto became known as "the Aryan side". Lena explained.

They put us in the ghetto and surrounded
the ghetto with a big wall, and the punishment

for entering or leaving the ghetto was death. But because there was not enough food delivered to the ghetto, there were some people that risked their lives to get food. The biggest heroes of the ghetto were little children who somehow found ways to smuggle themselves through the walls and to the other side. They either begged or swapped some things for food for the family. Some of the guards would try to catch a boy and if they found a carrot on him, or a piece of bread, or an onion or something they might let him go. But there were some sadists among them that just for a little carrot or a potato or something, they would shoot the boy.

Families saw their brothers and friends being killed for the big crime of bringing some food to their parents, to their families. The next day, those remaining were ready to risk their lives, and they went again. Somebody had to feed the family. They were the breadwinners of the family.

Jewish people were only permitted to bring the bare minimum with them, causing instant poverty. As there was little work, they exchanged whatever they could with other residents for food and other necessities. This caused a lot of hardship. In a tactic that appeared to be designed to bring about a slow death, the German administration deliberately limited food supplies to 253 calories a day, causing near starvation. Germans shot those who tried to escape and anyone who sheltered them.

Weakened by malnutrition, unsanitary conditions, lack of services, overpopulation and lack of medical care, there was a deadly outbreak of typhus. Tragically, 20 per cent of the entire population – 92,000 Jews in the Warsaw Ghetto – died between October 1940 and July 1942. They died of starvation, disease and the bitterly cold weather. Temperatures could be below zero in the winter months, and people were inadequately dressed, with no heating.

14. Homeless Children in Warsaw Ghetto

15. Working Jews Warsaw Ghetto

5

Life and Death in the Warsaw Ghetto

It was our fate, and we had to live with it.
—Lena Goldstein

Death hovered over the ghetto. Lena said, "You could not avoid touching passersby, and that caused a very bad epidemic of typhus. Typhus is, if you haven't got any medication like we didn't have, especially an antibiotic, it's a fatal disease. It transfers from one person to another just by one little louse. You'll find on you a louse and, if it's infected, then your lifespan was about two weeks. People were dying from typhus, a few hundred per day."

Lena describes the pervasive sense of resignation that swept the ghetto. "It was our fate, and we had to live with it. We got so used to corpses lying in the street covered with newspapers, we didn't think anything about it." Not thinking about it was how they coped.

Lena's best friend's sister had typhus. She didn't want her sister to go to the hospital. Lena and her friend risked their lives to look after her. They had to be very careful to wash the sheets, everything. She survived but, in a cruel twist of fate, the day after her recovery the Germans took her to a death camp where they gassed her.

The Germans set up a Jewish Council, or *Judenrat*, to administer their ghettos, and Jewish police to carry out their orders. This often put these Jews in a moral dilemma. They were responsible to their German masters but most didn't want to betray their people.

Jews from other nations had been transported into the Warsaw Ghetto as well, and the Germans had the support of the Polish Service, Lithuanians and Ukrainians in persecuting the Jews.

People were starving. When the announcement came that Jews in the Warsaw Ghetto who were willing to work for the Germans would be paid, not with money, but with food for the family and that their family would be safe, Lena's parents got a job in a German laundry. A large number of factories and facilities were set up in the ghetto with industries ironically and cruelly supplying the German war machine.

But how safe were they? In July 1942, a new "death camp" opened at Treblinka. This was to be the graveyard of the Jews of the Warsaw Ghetto. It was the last of four death camps built by the Nazis as part of the final solution for the Jews – mass extermination and genocide. Part of Operation Reinhard, the other camps, Chelmno, Belzec and Sobibor, were already in murderous operation. The Nazi plan was to kill all Polish Jews by the end of 1942.

Lena's boyfriend, Simon, was working in a factory in the ghetto making weapons for the Germans. The work was so precise they could only use engineers or watchmakers. He had studied law with Lena and then with the anti-Semitism at Warsaw University, he went to France and studied engineering. The Germans had already taken his parents to the death camp. Lena said, "He came to my factory [the laundry] to ask for my hand from my mother. He thought we would be safe because of his specialised job. I decided to stay with my parents and not save my life by marrying him. The Germans had said he would be safe. But they took him anyway." There was no trusting the Germans' assurances. It was a gut-wrenching decision. She loved Simon and missed him terribly but felt she needed to support her parents. Lena now believes that one of the miracles that helped her survive was staying with her parents.

Mass deportations from the ghetto begin

On 22 July the death sentence for Warsaw's Jews was issued. It was the eve of Tisha B'Av (9Av), 1942, the day the Jews had for centuries mourned the destruction of their first and second temples and the end of their political independence. So, it was ironical the Nazis would choose this day for the *Grossaktion*, or Great Action. At 7.30 am, the *Judenrat* received orders from the Resettlement Affairs authorities that all Jews residing in Warsaw would be resettled to the east, regardless of age or sex. This order would include children. Six thousand Jews per day had to be rounded up and deported. The *Judenrat* was shocked but was used to obeying orders.

Adam Czerniakow was the head the Jewish Community Council in Warsaw, and he continued under the German authorities when, on 3 October 1939, the twenty-four-member Jewish Council – the *Judenrat* – was made responsible for executing Nazi orders in the Jewish community. He tried hard to look after the welfare of the Jews in the Warsaw Ghetto under impossible conditions.

The Germans asked him to sign deportation orders for the children, and he tried frantically to have the orders reversed. Despite reassurances that the children would be spared, he realised how impossible a situation he was in, and committed suicide by swallowing cyanide pills. That he was in the habit of carrying these in his pocket shows this must have been on his mind for some time. He left a suicide note for his wife, Dr Felicia, who was being held hostage under threat of death to force him to sign the papers: "I am powerless, my heart trembles in sorrow and compassion. I can no longer bear all this." (Jewish Virtual Library 2018a)

He did not sign the order. His wife survived the war. Some saw him as brave and principled; others thought he was weak for not warning Jews in the ghetto about the impending disaster.

A notice by the *Judenrat* of the transportation to the east was posted with no signature. It mentioned exemptions for workers, so there was a frenzied rush to get work permits to work in the German factories, thinking this would make them safe. However, it was a calculated move by Nazis to get more workers for their war machine. The first to be taken were those in poorhouses, the sick in the streets and Jewish refugees from Germany, newly arrived. When Jewish police had a problem filling the numbers, the Germans broke into locked houses, firing over people's heads and pulling them out from hiding in cellars, chimneys and attics.

Over the next few days, the Germans transported hundreds of thousands of Jews to Treblinka death camp. Initially Jewish police had to round them up but then, after a week, about two hundred Ukrainian, Latvian and Lithuanian soldiers and German gendarmes took charge.

As the weeks went on, the Germans and their henchmen became more brutal and started taking a wider circle of people, such as the families of those with work permits. Then they began entering workplaces and catching Jews. It was an endless nightmare where Jews were beaten, shouted at and threatened with weapons.

The Germans tried a new tactic. A poster appeared, telling the Jews to go to the *Umschlagplatz* station where they would get three kilograms of bread and one kilogram of jam. The ploy worked as the children were starving. The Jews were told they were being transported to work camps. Thousands turned up.

On 6 August the Germans came to transport the children from the orphanage. Principal Janusz Korzak refused to save himself and stayed with the children keeping them calm. He went with them to his death and theirs, comforting them as best he could. Today, he is considered a hero for his sacrifice. Israel Gutman writes,

> Korzak lined his children up in rows of four. The orphans were clutching flasks of water and their favourite books and toys. They were in their best clothes. Korzak stood at the head of his 192 children, holding a child with each hand… They marched through the ghetto to the *Umschlagplatz* where they joined thousands of people waiting with no shade, water or shelter in the hot August

sun. The children did not cry out…a mute protest. (Gutman 2012)

Anxiety, desperation, fear and hunger were all taking their toll. The last massive selection began on the night of 6 September and lasted until 10 September. All Jews were to assemble in an area bounded by four streets and go through a selection process, leaving through a narrow path with Germans standing menacingly on each side with bayonets and whips. It was called the "Cauldron Decree" later, as they placed the Jews in an area the size of a cauldron. Only those with work permits (possessed by one-tenth of the ghetto at the beginning of the expulsion) were "safe" for the time being.

Those without numbers (permits) trudged off to their death. Crying babies carried by their parents through the cauldron were bayoneted mercilessly, including any bundles that could be hiding them.

A few Jews managed to escape Treblinka and bring news to the ghetto of the horrible truth that Treblinka was not a work camp but a death camp. The remaining Jews found it hard to believe that slaughter on such an industrial scale could occur. The Polish Underground investigated and found out the truth. However, there was little contact between the Polish Underground and the Jews of the Warsaw Ghetto.

Lena remembers Jewish New Year 1942, when there was an *Aktion* (Action), and Lena couldn't march with her parents because she was there illegally and didn't have papers, so she had to stay hiding. Lena said, "There was a big warehouse where the uniforms were coming to be washed, and I was hiding there under those uniforms, and with me was an elderly Jewish gentleman, Mr Lauterstein. His family was also working in the laundry, but he was too old to work already. I was not too old, but I just couldn't get the job. When we came out, the *Aktion* was over and…" Her voice trails off. "But now I'm so emotional, I forget words. What was it called when they were choosing this one to the other?"

"Selection," Eva helped her out.

"Yes, selection, "said Lena. "The Germans had promised those with jobs wouldn't be taken. Anyway, those taken kept little children in suitcases, giving them sleeping tablets so they wouldn't be separated. The selection was finished, and people were gone, and we came out from under the piles of uniforms. My father was there. My mother was gone. And the whole family of the old man that was hiding with me was taken away. I never saw my mother again, and the old man never saw his family again."

Lena stares into space for a while. As a young woman, she was powerless to do anything about it when the German killing machine swung into action. She pushed down the feelings of grief and devastation. "My mother was gone. I was so used to everything, I didn't cry. We were waiting for our turn."

Though she was heartbroken, Lena had to muster the will to survive. She started working in place of her mother and receiving food as payment. She needed a ration of food to survive. It was only once a day, and it was just a bowl of cabbage soup. Lena said, "If we were lucky, there was a leaf of cabbage in it. If we were extremely lucky, we could even find a piece of potato in the soup. And I can't remember now whether it was 100 or 150 grams of bread, and that was our food for the whole day. Because I started working instead of my mother, I was getting a portion, and my father was getting a portion. The old man was not getting any food at all. So, my father divided those two portions into three and shared it with the old man, and took care of him. You know, he couldn't even speak Polish, so my father spoke Yiddish to him."

In a cruel mockery, the Nazis would choose Jewish religious festivals to strike. The next *Aktion* was on *Yom Kippur*, the Day of Atonement, nearly two weeks later. The Germans forced the Jews to march, deciding who would be transported to Treblinka camp and who would stay. Lena said, "I was marching with my father. Because I was already a working girl and the old man couldn't work. They sent my father to Treblinka to the left and me to the right. I ran after my father. I didn't want to be all alone. I was badly beaten with whips. I don't know how I got back to the laundry. They dragged me back. Except that my father was gone, the old man was gone, and I was left alone."

Bruised and battered, Lena could only crumple up in a corner. Starving, she took a bite of bread for some comfort. *Yom Kippur* is a day of fasting. Lena looks back through time. "It was the day they took my father. I didn't cry. A man praying saw me with a piece of bread and said, 'See it's because of you, God's punishing us.' I caused it!" she said indignantly. "The Holocaust was because I had a piece of bread," she said, her raised eyebrows and ironic tone sweeping away this accusation. She would not accept the guilt and her disgust at that accusation has remained with her to this day.

"Chosen people," she muses. "Why doesn't God choose someone else?"

This reminds me of the famous scene in *Fiddler on the Roof*, when Tevye, a poor Jewish farmer in difficulty in Ukraine, says to God, "I know, I know, we are the chosen people. But once in a while can't you choose somebody else?"

****

The *Aktions*, or deportations, occurred between 22 July and 21 September 1942 (the Day of Atonement, the holiest day in Judaism). This reduced the ghetto to 50,000 to 60,000 people, mostly men between fifteen and fifty years old. It lasted for about sixty hellish days with 265,000 Jews transported to their death at Treblinka, 11,580 sent to forced labour camps and about 10,000 murdered in the streets either for resisting or just for sport. About 8000 managed to escape to the Aryan side.

16. Umschlagplatz, Warsaw Ghetto

17. Umschlagplatz, Warsaw Ghetto Deportation

6

Remember Me:
Treblinka Death Camp

Some were screaming to heaven – "God look at us, help us!" I didn't lose my faith because I was not very faithful before that. My parents were traditional Jews but, after what I saw, maybe I should believe in miracles.

—Lena Goldstein

"Someone told me my father was saying *Kaddish* and leading prayer in Treblinka. Before being taken, he was only worried about me." Lena rubs her eyes and ears a few times, although I can't see any tears. "He was saying *Kaddish* not for the ones who were dead already but for the ones going into the gas chambers. Some were screaming to heaven – 'God look at us, help us!' My parents were traditional Jews but, after what I saw, maybe I should believe in miracles. Some Jews were given away as children to Poles. Poles who helped Jews were shot together with them, along with their children," said Lena. "Some Jews lost their faith, and some didn't."

Lena didn't know at the time the horror her parents, and the others who were taken with them to Treblinka, faced. They were herded onto trains, the doors locked behind them – crammed in like cattle, standing room only, for a journey that took hours, with no food, no drink, no toilets. They could hardly breathe, with just a few small windows on the trains. Some women vomited with the smell. Mothers clung to crying children, trying to comfort them. Some people had hidden a few valuables and had a small suitcase with them, hoping they could make a new life, although their hearts were breaking for loved ones left behind. They were tormented by thirst and filled with a dreadful foreboding. The Germans told them they were going to labour camps in the east. Treblinka was near the railroad junction of the village of Malkinia Górna.

Did it rain that day to hide the tears of those ripped from the arms of loved ones and being driven to their death? Did the earth refuse to bear the burden of human cargo, rising to stop the train in its tracks, forbidding it to go forward? Did the wind howl with sorrow or wail with despair? Did the trees of the forest, some almost touching the train, extend their branches like helping hands?

More Jews were killed at Auschwitz by the Nazis than anywhere else – estimates range from 1.1 million to 1.5 million. However, Treblinka was next, with between 700,000 and 900,000 murdered. These are shocking figures to contemplate. About six million Jews met their death in the genocide of the Holocaust, 1.5 million of these being children.

The forced deportation of Jews from the Warsaw Ghetto had started on 22 July 1942 with thousands transported daily to the new extermination camp at Treblinka, in Poland. On 18 July, Heinrich Himmler, head of the Nazi SS, ordered the Warsaw Ghetto emptied and the Jews sent to the death camp at Treblinka, about 100 kilometres north-east of Warsaw. More than 250,000 Jews were gassed to death in the first seven weeks of Himmler's order. This made it World War Two's largest single act of destruction of any population group, Jewish or non-Jewish, civilian or military.

As the train approached Treblinka, the Jews saw Poles working in the fields and called out to them, asking if they knew their fate. Some of the Poles looked up long enough to shout "death" and terror seized the Jews. They couldn't believe it. The train lurched on, passing through recently dug-up forest. The train approached the large gate of Treblinka, the gates of hell, and the wagons were shunted in towards a ramp, the train escorts being commanded to stay outside as the camp guards took over. The SS, with guns, hand-grenades and rubber truncheons, awaited the passengers. It was an alarming sight for those who could see through the small windows. They shouted their impressions to the others, who were startled but barely standing. Suddenly the wagon doors flung open and the Jews were driven out onto the ramp. Some fainted, many gasped for breath, others screamed and wailed. Children cried, searching for their parents.

The SS rushed at the group, forcing them to hurry. The sick and elderly begged for help and a squad wearing Red Cross armbands took them, including children without parents, on stretchers if necessary, to the *Lazarett*, or infirmary. There they were made to strip and sit on a long bench facing a fire. They were mercilessly machine-gunned in the back of the head, and fell into the fire.

Wielding truncheons, the SS herded the others through a gate and into a square surrounded with barbed wire interwoven with leafy branches to camouflage it. Women were commanded to go to the right and men to the left. They resisted, the SS driving them apart as heartbreaking farewells rang out. Husbands were separated from wives, sons from their mothers, and daughters from their fathers, brothers from their sisters. Their pain and their thirst were overwhelming.

Then came the humiliating order to undress. Jewish slaves gave them red string to tie their shoes together to save sorting them afterwards. Embarrassed, many women covered their breasts with their arms. Those taking too long to undress for the so-called showers were beaten. Jewish slaves cut the women's hair in one rough cut and immediately put the locks into sacks. Everything the Jews owned was harvested for the German war machine. After they were killed, the gold would be extracted from their teeth. Ironically, the Jews had to fund their own demise.

The men were made to run around the square many times to exhaust them and lower their resistance to the death camp. As they were driven towards their deaths, some men were pulled out at the last minute to join work squads. For now, their lives were spared but much horror and deprivation awaited them. There were many squads. The blue squad with blue armbands had to clear the trains of dead bodies and human waste. The red squad carried the sick and weak to the infirmary. There were many other squads – squads to sort clothes and valuables, camouflage squads to hide the camp with fresh branches daily, the squad that took the bodies from the gas chambers and buried them and many more. It was like a mini city needing shoemakers, carpenters and so on.

The sorting squad had to check clothes carefully to see if valuables had been sewn into the lining. So much was plundered from the Jews that lorries were needed to transport gold, the only item they carried. There were also transports that carried silk dresses only or men's suits only. It didn't all go to the German government. The SS became personally very rich and, on their leave, took suitcases of the best jewellery and clothes for their families.

Economic plunder of the Jews was part of the Nazi plan. Nearly 120 billion Reich marks – over £12 billion at the time – was plundered from German Jews by laws and looting (Hall 2010). By today's figures, that would be many billions of dollars. The same research study says the Jews paid for about one-third of Germany's war effort. That doesn't take into account their slave labour. This is an incredible irony considering they were the chief target of this war.

The Third Reich plundered the Jews via taxes, taking their properties and businesses, and robbing dead bodies. Jewish *Sonderkommandos* were forced to use pliers to yank gold teeth out of the mouths of the dead. According to William Shirer's book, *The Rise and Fall of the Third Reich*, the quantity of dental gold sent to Berlin filled up three huge vaults at the Reichbank and the Nazis had to store the rest of it in abandoned salt mines (Quora 2017). This was just gold teeth, let alone the vast quantities of gold in coins and jewellery the Nazis stole.

A forced labour camp called Treblinka I had been set up near a gravel pit in June 1941 so, when the death camp was set up in July 1942, it was known as Treblinka II or T11. Treblinka 1 was a forced-labour camp (*Arbeitslager*) whose slave labourers worked in the gravel pit, irrigation area or forest, where they cut wood to fuel the cremation pits. Over half of its 20,000 inmates died by execution, hunger or disease.

Trees were used to camouflage the barbed wire that surrounded Treblinka, and it had watchtowers. Amazingly only twenty-five German SS were required to run the camp. There were living quarters for the Nazis and about one hundred Ukrainian guards, and another section for the one thousand Jewish slave labourers, including those who removed clothes and valuables from the victims beforehand and disposed of their bodies afterwards, making the gas chambers spotless after each trainload. They had to clean it in five to ten minutes, disposing of papers and pots and pans the people had with them so the next group would not be suspicious. It was gut-wrenching work.

The first commandant of TII, was Dr Irmfried Eberl, aged thirty-two, "the man who had headed up the euthanasia program of 1940 and had much experience with the gassing of victims, especially children" (History.com 2009). Jewish prisoners were killed as soon as they outlived their usefulness or at the whim of their masters. "Eberl was relieved of his duties for 'inefficiency'. It seems that he and his workers could not remove the corpses quickly enough, and panic was occurring within the railway cars of newly arrived prisoners." (History.com 2009)

Such evil can't be explained or understood. Hitler successfully promoted the theory that the Jews were the reason for all their problems and a final solution was needed to rid Europe of them so that Germany's problems, economic and otherwise, would be solved. He misused the word "Aryan" to describe his idea of a pure German race, or *Herrenvolk*, which he regarded as superior to all other races. He was obsessed with the idea of racial purity.

Anti-Semitism had been fanned for generations by the Catholic Church, as Jews had been accused of being Christ-killers. Even the famed Martin Luther, who started the Reformation, had turned against Jews when they refused to be converted, imbuing the Lutheran Church with anti-Semitism. Hitler's demonic idea to murder every Jew in Europe could not have succeeded without the underlying anti-Semitism and racial prejudice in Europe of Christians and others.

Hitler's racial imperialism and plan to create *Lebensraum*, or living space, for the Germans led to his strategy to kill or enslave all Slavic populations, who were considered *Untermensch* (subhuman) and populate the land with Germans. As the Wehrmacht (armed forces of Nazi Germany) swept across Poland, the plan was to make it *Judenrein*, or cleansed of Jews.

Using bullets to kill Jews was not quick enough, used too much manpower and rattled some who had to do it. A conference was held to plan Hitler's Final Solution on 20 January 1942, at Wannsee, a suburb of Berlin. Head of the Reich Security Main Office (RSHA), SS General Reinhard Heydrich, ran the meeting. Adolf Eichmann wrote the protocols, which included the words "transportation to the East", a euphemism for the genocide of Europe's Jews, who numbered about eleven million at the time. Josef Bühler, State Secretary of the General Government of occupied Poland, asked for the Final Solution to occur in Poland because transportation was not a problem. About 1,700,000 Jews were killed in Operation Reinhard.

Aktion (Action) Reinhard was the name given to the plan to send Jews to their deaths at Treblinka, and the other extermination camps built in Poland – Belzec and Sobibor. According to the Central Commission for Investigation of German Crimes in Poland, a fourth death camp had already opened at Chelmno, today's Poland. The Nazis gassed the first Jews there in mobile vans on 8 December 1941. (Scapbookpages.com 1998)

The three Operation Reinhard camps were all located near the Bug River on the eastern border of German-occupied Poland. Belarus, or White Russia, was on the other side of the river. It had been part of Poland but had been given to the Soviet Union after the Germans and Soviets invaded Poland in September 1939. The Germans advanced into Russia and planned to transport Russian Jews to the Bug River, gas them and claim they had been transported to the east.

The first Jews sent to the Treblinka extermination camp were from Lena's Warsaw Ghetto. Records show:

> ...the first transport of 6,000 Jews arrived
> at Treblinka at about 9:30 on 23 July 1942.
> Between late July and September 1942, the
> Germans transported more than 300,000 Jews
> from the Warsaw ghetto to Treblinka, according
> to the US Holocaust Memorial Museum. Jews
> were also deported to Treblinka from Lublin and
> Bialystok, two major cities in eastern Poland,
> which were then in the General Government, as
> German-occupied Poland was called. Others were
> transported to Treblinka from the Theresienstadt
> Ghetto in what is now the Czech Republic.
> Approximately 2,000 Gypsies were also sent to
> Treblinka and murdered in the gas chambers.
> (Scapbookpages.com 1998)

The Germans sent Jews from Poland, Austria, Belgium,
Czechoslovakia, France, Greece, Yugoslavia, Germany and the Soviet
Union to Treblinka. Other estimates are that 330,000 Jews from the
Warsaw Ghetto died there. The uprising at the Warsaw Ghetto that
was to follow lasted nearly a month, and 7000 died fighting. Those
who survived were rounded up and sent to Treblinka. The Nazis
transported many Jews in cattle cars like animals, others in crowded
passenger trains that could hold 3000 people and even horse-drawn
wagons and trucks. Trains arrived regularly at Treblinka until May
1943 with only a few after that.

When the Jews arrived at Treblinka, they saw a fake railway
station with destination signs, a ticket office, timetables and a clock
designed to trick them into thinking that they were at a transit camp
on their way to the east. But it was a storehouse where workers would
put the clothes of the Jews once they had stripped as ordered. Yet,
despite this attempt to keep the Jews calm and unaware of their fate
on arrival, suspicions were alerted at the odour of decaying bodies,
which could be smelled up to ten kilometres away.

Oskar Berger, who escaped during the 1943 uprising, remembered the horrifying sights of Treblinka on arrival in August 1942:

> When we were unloaded, we noticed a paralyzing view – all over the place, there were hundreds of human bodies. Piles of packages, clothes, suitcases, everything was in a mess. German and Ukrainian SS-men stood at the corners of the barracks and were shooting blindly into the crowd. (Chrostowski 2004)

Jewish men faced the heartbreak of sometimes having to cut the hair of loved ones. Abraham Bomba was a Jewish barber who had to cut their hair at Treblinka before they were gassed. He described the concrete gas chambers, with two steel doors, one on each side, and wires on the top looking like water would come out of them. He told his story to the US Holocaust Memorial Museum:

> When it was full the gas chamber – the size of it was… I would say 18 by 18, or 18 by 17… And they pushed in as many as they could. It was not allowed to have the people standing up with their hands down because there is not enough room, but when people raised their hand like that, there was more room for each other. And on top of that, they throw in kids, 2, 3, 4 years old kids, on top of them. (Scapbookpages.com 1998)

He estimated it took seven minutes at the most. Those who worked in Treblinka II only handled the dead, so it was their job to open the door on the opposite side to where the people had entered and remove their bodies, although a few were still alive. They were dragged to the ditches and unceremoniously covered up.

It was an industrial killing machine. Estimates are that the Nazis killed about 10,000 to 12,000 people daily. With Nazi efficiency, the whole process took about two hours from the arrival of a train until the disposal of the bodies. There were two undressing huts, one for men and one for women. They had to undress in subzero temperatures. If they resisted, they were stabbed. Then the door was sealed and the gas poured in through openings like cones. Screams rang out. The Nazis kept up the charade that the Jews were to be disinfected in the showers. The mental anguish of the prisoners was immense, having to continually watch this procession of those doomed to destruction.

Those who didn't cooperate on arrival were whipped and forced to run naked through a tube or funnel to a building that had a sign on it that it was a shower room. Incredibly, the Nazis called this path to the gas chamber *Himmelfahrtstrasse*, or Street to Heaven. Samuel Rajzman testified to this at the Nuremberg Trials, saying that another ten gas chambers were added to the original three as the killing was sped up. Diesel engines pumped carbon monoxide into the gas chambers. Some say the diesel engines were obtained from captured Russian submarines. According to the Nizkor Project, large 500 BHP engines from captured Soviet T-34 tanks were used. Zyklon B, a deadly cyanide-based pesticide was used at Auschwitz-Birkenau but not Treblinka. At Treblinka the bodies were at first buried in large pits and then later dug up and burnt.

The Germans were so comfortable with what they were doing that Commandant Frank Franz built a zoo of captured forest animals like foxes, which was surrounded by pine trees and birches, where the SS could relax. It even had exotic birds. There was a beer garden with tables and sunshades for them to unwind after a hard day's killing. Flower beds were planted and colourful paint was used on buildings to brighten up their living space. The SS men jogged on nature trails and swam in the Bug River.

There was entertainment for SS staff and some of the privileged prisoners, called *Kapos*. Some SS had their families there, and they dressed up for special events. Polish Jews who were forced to build Treblinka were also required to play music for them during meals and in the evenings. When Artur Gold was sent there from the Warsaw Ghetto, he was ordered to set up an orchestra to entertain them. Songs were created in the camp by Jews. The bitterly ironic lyrics of the "Treblinka song", written by Commandant Kurt Franz, called upon prisoners to keep their "gaze forwards, always brave and happy" (Music and the Holocaust n.d.). Prisoners not killed on arrival but put to forced labour were required to learn it on their first day. A ten-man orchestra was forced to play during the day near the gas chambers to distract the SS from the screams of the dying.

It was not just backbreaking but heartbreaking work for the Jews who, snatched from the jaws of death, were forced to work for the German death machine. Nightmares plagued them in the camp, and, for those few who survived, continued to plague them as they tried desperately to return to normal lives. Some chose suicide in TII rather than serve the Germans and a few survivors could not live with themselves afterwards and chose to take their lives. A few survivors of the various camps experienced survivor guilt that they had survived and not others. Many experienced an obsession with hoarding food after the war because hoarding food such as a scrap of bread or a potato had been the only way to survive when they were starving and food was scarce. Treblinka was not liberated by the Americans but when Americans fed emaciated liberated Jews after the war, some tragically died because their bodies couldn't handle the food.

Besides the millions of Jews slaughtered in concentration camps, there were tens of thousands of captured soldiers, political prisoners, gypsies and homosexuals. In 1942, the Nazis decided that forced labourers in these death camps would work harder if they could get sex, so they forced female prisoners into brothels. When women were worn out, many were killed, and there were forced sterilisations and abortions. Many male prisoners were too exhausted or lacked the finance to use the brothels, as the Germans required a small payment. The Nazis also forced male homosexuals to use the brothels to "cure" them. Jewish women were not used in the brothels because of "racial hygiene", and Jewish men did not have access to them (Fallet and Kaiser 2009). All over Europe during World War Two, there were

German military brothels, and it is estimated that the Nazis forced over 34,000 women into sexual slavery. Treblinka was not one of the camps where there were brothels.

A special SS training camp at Trawniki, Poland, trained more than 5000 Ukrainian soldiers of the Red Army (some were ex-prisoners of war) so they could help the Germans achieve the Final Solution. They were also used to quell the Warsaw Ghetto uprising and other ghetto revolts. (Black 2006)

Kurt Franz was the last camp commandant of Treblinka, serving from mid-August until November 1943. As he had a baby-like face, he was nicknamed *Lalke* (doll in Yiddish) by the prisoners. However, he was particularly sadistic. He would often make his rounds of the camp riding a horse and would often command his dog Barry to bite the genitalia or buttocks of the prisoners, sometimes mauling them mercilessly. Franz would issue a dehumanising command as if the Jew were the dog and his dog a person: "Man, get that dog!" (deathcamps. org 2006)

He warned ten prisoners would be shot for every escapee or escape attempt. Franz enjoyed shooting prisoners or those still in the trains as they arrived. He would interrogate bearded men on arrival if they believed in God and, if so, would shoot them. Cruelly, Franz also relished kicking and killing babies as they arrived off the trains.

18. Treblinka Death Camp in Summer 1945

19. Train from Warsaw Ghetto Arrives at Treblinka August 1942

7

Lena Joins the Resistance
in the Ghetto

*All the others were already gone, so there were flats
with nobody there, and that was my other function,
to unscrew the light bulbs because from the light
bulbs they were making Molotov cocktails. And the
Molotov cocktails, they're using against the German
tanks. The Molotov cocktails had kerosene in them,
and then they light them, and they are like a bomb,
like a hand grenade.*

—Lena Goldstein

After the deportations, the ghetto was a ghost town. The Jews mourned
the loss of loved ones. While they were shocked, angry and exhausted,
they also felt guilty and were filled with self-questioning. The youth
were demoralised and there were recriminations. Why hadn't there
been resistance – spontaneous or organised?

Emanuel Ringelblum, a Jewish historian who recorded ghetto
history in the *Oneg Shabbat* Archive, wrote of a number of reasons,
in summary: the element of surprise used by the Germans; their use
of Jews as accessories (police and *Judenrat*) as a deterrent to resistance;
the difficulty of getting food into the ghetto; and the gradual selection process masking the scale of it. Further, he surmised that the

combination of these factors led to a breakdown of community and the "war of all against all for survival". (Gutman 2012)

I would add to these reasons the deception used by the Germans, that they were going to work camps not death camps, that workers and their families would be protected, and the Germans' use of food to entice starving families.

Jewish police were active and even brutal throughout the expulsions, and they were reviled by angry ghetto residents afterwards. Some Jewish police left the force, forgoing the protection it offered them, and didn't take part in the deportations. Jewish police were treated better by the Germans for their service but were also pressured by the Germans that, if they didn't provide the numbers for transportation, their families would be taken. Ironically, as a reward, the police were the last to be expelled on 12 September 1942, although some remained. Accounts vary as to whether this was 12 or 21 September.

About 35,000 Jews received permission to remain in the ghetto as essential workers and were placed in living areas allotted to the workplaces. There were three enclaves and communication between them was forbidden. An extra 20,000 were in hiding as illegal residents.

The Jewish Fighting Organisation (ZOB) was formed by Yitzhak Zuckerman (called Antek), Joseph Kaplan and Mordechai Tennenbaum-Tamarof in July, about a week after the deportations began, but it had no weapons or strategy and no contact with the outside world. Polish communists gave them some weapons but the Germans confiscated them and killed Kaplan and another leader.

When Mordechai Anielewicz heard of the expulsions from the ghetto, he went there and, not being burdened by the feelings of failure of some of the Jews who weren't taken, acted decisively to restore confidence and develop partnerships with those who could help, like the Gordonia movement. Its leader Eliezer Geller and his friends returned to the ghetto after the expulsions to work with ZOB.

The Polish underground didn't provide much help to the Jews until after the great deportations. They did manage to smuggle some children out and find homes for them. Only ten pistols and a small amount of ammunition were given to ZOB by *Armia Krajowa* (AK,

the Polish underground army) in December 1942. This poor equip-
ping reflected the indifference of many Poles to Jews because they
were considered social outsiders or "not one of us".

However, a coordinating committee was established for the
Jewish underground and ZOB to speak with the Polish underground.
Unity between Jewish groups, which had been so difficult to achieve,
was forming. However, the revisionist organisation, Betar, a right-
wing group, formed the Jewish Fighting Union (ZZW) rather than
join ZOB, which was more left wing. ZZW was headed up by Pavel
Frenkel, Dawid Apfelbaum, Leon Rodal and Dawid Wdowinski
(political chair), among others.

Jan Karski, a representative of the Polish underground was sent to
London to report on the situation in Poland. He saw two Jews first –
Leon Feiner of the *Bund* and Ariel Wilner of the Zionists. Karski saw
officials and Jewish leaders in London and went to the US, speaking
with President Roosevelt and at many meetings throughout the country. So, the world knew the plight of the Jews of Poland. There was
therefore no excuse for the lack of support for the dying Polish Jews.

Henryk Wolinski helped set up *Zegota*, or the Council to Aid the
Jews, in autumn 1942. It answered to the Polish government in exile
and was the only organisation run by Jews and Poles during World
War Two. *Zegota* helped save about 4000 Jews by providing food,
medical care, false identity documents and relief money for those hiding on the Aryan side. Some had escaped from work camps, deportation trains and ghettos. Between the Jewish National Committee, the
Bund and *Zegota*, about 8500 of the 28,000 Jews hiding in Warsaw
were helped, as well as about 1000 Jews in other parts of Poland.

***

Groups of young people worked with the resistance in the ghetto
and Lena wanted to join them. "They didn't want to accept me with
the resistance as there was not enough money for revolvers. We would
be fighting against tanks and aeroplanes and heavy artillery that the
Germans had. They couldn't afford to buy revolvers, which weren't

so easy to get anyway. They wouldn't accept a young girl like me who couldn't shoot."

The resistance gave Lena an assignment, however. There was a 7 pm curfew. She had a flat to herself because the Germans had deported the others to Treblinka. The apartment was in a block and was one room only, not just one bedroom. So, the young people in the resistance could stay overnight at Lena's. At 7 am, after people went to work, they came out in black jackets and black masks because their identity had to be kept secret, even from Jews. They asked for money from Jews they knew would be sympathetic.

Lena was still working in the laundry, and the resistance gave her the job of the "courier" of the uniforms, carrying them on her shoulders. They wanted her to steal German uniforms. Lena spoke about it:

> We didn't have vans to take the uniforms to the factories to repair. We had to carry them on our shoulders. There was a whole street of those factories, and the boys from the Jewish fighting organisation were hiding behind the entrance to the next house. They were pulling uniforms off my shoulders one at a time.
>
> I was going there a few times a day. You couldn't take off more than one because it would show and then I would come there, and they would ask, "Where are the uniforms?" It wasn't even dangerous because they were pulling one at a time and nobody saw that one was missing. There were always some of the uniforms that were damaged and couldn't be returned, so it was not hard to explain. We had to wash them and dry them and then we took them back but, you know, we would go there about five, six, seven times a day.
>
> I thought that it was a stupid idea. Why do they give me an order like that? Who needs

German uniforms? After leaving the ghetto, I heard that all the fighters of the Jewish uprising were wearing German uniforms. And the Germans didn't know whether they were shooting a friend or a foe, so I hope that helped them. You know, a few hundred young boys, mostly boys, were fighting against this mighty German army for a whole month.

There were many empty flats because the Germans had transported the occupants to Treblinka death camp. Lena had a habit of euphemising it by saying they had been "taken". Perhaps using that language at the time protected the Jews a little from the trauma happening daily around them. The resistance gave Lena another way of helping the Warsaw Ghetto Uprising. She said, "The place with the flat I was living in had three families there. After a while, I was the only one left there. All the others were already gone, so there were flats with nobody there, and that became my other function, to unscrew the light bulbs. From the light bulbs they were making Molotov cocktails to use against German tanks. The Molotov cocktails had kerosene in them, and then they light them, and they were like a bomb, like a hand grenade. So that was my other job."

Lena remembers the well-known Holocaust song written by a poet in her flat in the ghetto. It is called *Where Can I Go?* This was the experience of many Jews as they sought safety and felt no one wanted them.

8

A Miracle Escape
from the Ghetto

*If I have to die tomorrow, I'm not going to wash
their uniforms today. And because I didn't want to
go to Treblinka and be poisoned, I would rather be
killed on the spot here.*

–Lena Goldstein

It was Easter 1943, and by then out of 450,000 people who went into
the ghetto, there were about 35,000 left alive, working. Lena sensed
her time was up.

> And Passover is coming, another holiday, so
> we knew that now they'll come with, you know,
> the selection and they will kill the rest of us. And
> I decided that, if I have to die tomorrow, I'm not
> going to wash their uniforms today. Because I
> didn't want to go to Treblinka and be poisoned, I
> would rather be killed on the spot here.
> So, I got dressed in my best, whatever that
> meant, and, instead of going to work, I went for
> a walk. Around the ghetto was a big wall but
> there are little factories. A whole street was full
> of factories. So that was surrounded by a smaller

wall. Guards were standing at the smaller wall, and then there was a bigger wall surrounding the whole ghetto, and there were guards there too.

Anyway, I went for a walk right in front of the guards that were guarding our street there but, instead of shooting me, they called me, and they offered me a cigarette. And I said, "No, thank you. I don't smoke."

So, they took out the whole packet to give it to me and said, "Give it to your boyfriend."

"My boyfriend isn't alive anymore," I said.

"'That's what we wanted to talk to you about. We will be starting an *Aktion* in a few days' time. We'll be starting on the big wall. You go home and bleach your hair because Poles are Slavs and Slavs are blond. We'll recognise you and let you go to the Aryan side."

They were risking their lives to say that if somebody was eavesdropping and overheard, because helping a Jew was the same punishment as what they would give the Jew. They would kill someone who tried to save a Jew. So, I was really, very, very much touched by it. There were some nice Germans. They must have talked about wanting to save someone.

I went home that night, and I thought, you know, if somebody would have heard it, they risked their lives to help me. But I thought I wouldn't go to the Aryan side because I didn't have anybody there. Where will I go? I haven't got any money to pay for whatever I would have to pay and, besides, my younger brother came back when he was working in another factory, and we couldn't even get in touch because a wall also surrounded his factory. But he was here, sentenced to death.

I felt guilty that I would try to save myself that way. But when I came home, there was a slip of paper under the door.

The timing was amazing. Mr Lauterstein, the old man whom Lena's father had looked after, feeding him after he lost his whole family in the ghetto, had a son, a son-in-law and a granddaughter who somehow had escaped death. Lena described what happened:

> The old man must have told them how my father took care of him and that he would have died of starvation without the help he was given. They were hiding on the Aryan side in a bathroom of a flat of a caretaker for a big block of flats in Warsaw. So, in this bathroom they wrote that you could squeeze in another person there.
>
> They didn't know my name. They only knew where I lived so they had somehow smuggled a piece of paper that if the daughter of Mr Midler would like to join them, they would be very happy to have me there with them in hiding. That was not a 100 per cent security, but it was at least a way of trying to escape.
>
> I didn't think about it as something serious though. I didn't want to leave my brother there in danger, but I thought I would have to show it to my brother, just to show how people showed their gratitude that way. This was far more than gratitude. Because they risked their lives as well, you know. They already had their safety and to add another person was another reason for danger, and then to send the note was a danger too.

Lena recalls thinking that a piece of bread and soup could save a life and she would have to show her brother how people reacted to a good deed. It wasn't safe to walk on the streets so Lena stealthily made her way, climbing through the attics and cellars and through the walls, to find her brother. She bypassed hanging washing and stumbled on the hidden weapons of the resistance fighters.

Lena said feathers were useful to hide weapons. "People were trying to sell anything of worth to get some food, and the best way to get food was to sell bedding. They were only selling the outer part of the doona. There were so many feathers in the attic you couldn't see. I could go into the attic, and I wouldn't see you sitting there because there were so many feathers."

Lena finally found her brother Salek. He hugged her anxiously, knowing how dangerous it was for her to visit him. For a moment she relaxed into her brother's arms. He was the only family she had left. In trepidation, she showed him the letter that could spell her freedom and told him about the guards. It was risky but it might work. However, she couldn't leave him.

She said, "I'm not going. I can't leave you."

Salek was no longer wearing a suit and tie, and he no longer had the clean-shaven, neat hairstyle she was used to seeing. He looked weary. Salek looked at her kindly but spoke sternly, "No, you have to go. First of all, we can't help each other here because I'm dying when I hear that they've got Actions in your factory and I can't do anything for you, and you can't do anything for me. That's one thing, and the other thing is that they're going to kill the lot of us. And they will not want to tell the world what is going on here and nobody will believe it anyway. And the fact is that, even if you have eyewitnesses who were here, there are so many people who won't believe these horrors ever happened. Anyway, it is our duty to try to survive any way we can, just so that somebody has to tell the world what's happening here."

Lena's eyes searched his and saw the seriousness there. Salek held her close, realising he might never see his sister again. He added, "And, besides, somebody has to find out whether our sister is alive in

Siberia somewhere and somebody has to tell her what happened to our family."

The words of her brother have stayed with her and remain a large part of who she is, even today, seventy-five years later. Lena nodded and clung to him for a while. Lena's sobs were buried too deep to erupt. She loved him, and she also realised that she might never see him again. She slowly made her way back through the attics of feathers and hidden weapons.

Lena sat in her flat a while plucking up the courage to face the guards and go into the unknown. She didn't have the money for hair dye but she got dressed as well as she could, so she didn't look like a "poor Jewish washerwoman". She placed her only important possessions in the world in her handbag – six family photos and her two German passports.

Lena's heart was beating fast. Would those two Germans who offered to help be there? Or did someone overhear them and turn them in? What if some cruel guards were there instead? Would it matter that she hadn't dyed her hair blond? Would she be shot on the spot?

"And who should be standing there manning the big wall but my two German friends. And, stupid me, I took documents so that if someone else had been on the wall, it would be a giveaway. Anyone else would have asked me to open my bag, and in it I had documents and the photos of my family."

Lena wondered if they would remember her or had they changed their minds. Maybe they had just been playing a cruel game with her. Her stomach was churning and she was trying not to hold her breath in anticipation. They remembered. "And I just came, and they just let me through."

"Go." They waved her on to freedom. Lena was relieved and hurried on before they changed their minds. She couldn't believe they had spared her, that suddenly she was on the outside. But she held the tears back. Only a sigh of relief was allowed to escape.

In trepidation, but trying to look like she belonged, she found freedom on the Aryan side. But it wasn't safe. Who could she trust? She needed to get to her hiding place as soon as possible. With just the clothes on her back, her documents and photos, she hurriedly made her way to safety – no time to curiously look around to see the devastation of the war. She tried to avoid the rubble and avert her eyes from the destruction lest she betrayed her surprise at the scene.

In all the world, there was nowhere to go except to a group of strangers and hide with them in a confined space in a bathroom. She had no family to visit, no money, no clothes, no job, and she had left behind her flat and a few possessions in the ghetto, knowing that to stay would mean death.

****

Lena has shared her story many times now, so she presents it matter-of-factly. However, telling her story has helped her to cope with her memories and to process them. "So, I went and joined the family in the bathroom." She knocked quietly at the door of the large block of flats. The caretaker, aware she was coming, ushered her in with little fanfare. She was to hide now in a confined space for eighteen months with people she had not met before.

Whenever Lena tells her story, she reflects on these two acts of kindness. First, that of her father towards an old man he didn't know, a deed that allowed Lena a chance to escape from the ghetto. Second, that of two German soldiers who inexplicably allowed her, even encouraged her, to get away, despite all that was happening around them and the risks to themselves.

She joined Adek, the son-in-law of the old man, Mr Lauterstein. With Adek was his wife's brother Jacob (Jake) and niece Helen (Hela). They slept in sleeping bags in the bathroom. Mr Lauterstein's daughter and granddaughter had been killed.

Adek had been one of the first ones to come back and tell the Jews of Warsaw Ghetto about Treblinka. He had come home from work one day and found his wife and daughter gone. He followed them to Treblinka, thinking it was a work camp, but the Germans had already gassed his wife and child. He was distraught. However, he was blond and blue-eyed, which may have had a part to play in his outcome, and was chosen to deal with the people arriving at Treblinka. The Germans ordered them to take their clothes off. Adek had to collect the clothes, valuables and money. Lena explained:

> But workers like him were shot after two weeks. Knowing that was to be his end, he and three others decided to escape – to hide in the wagon under the clothing that they gathered, and on its way back to Germany they would pass Warsaw, and they would jump and go back to the ghetto. That's what they did, except after they jumped Adek never saw the others again. He didn't know what happened to them, whether they killed themselves by jumping or if they were caught. Adek himself was captured by a group of Polish youngsters, and they wanted to take him to the Gestapo. But he begged them first to take him to the mayor of this village, and they did.
>
> There was money, and some jewellery in the clothing of the people sent to Treblinka. The escaping men put some money into their pockets while preparing themselves to jump so that they would have something to pay for things. So, he went to this mayor. He took all the money that he had in his pocket, put it there on the table and said, "It's all yours if you'll allow me to go back to Warsaw." Not only did he allow him to go back to Warsaw, but he also allowed him to shave and to shower in his home. He gave him a suit because he had only the camp attire. And he went with him to the train and was sitting next to him to give him a little bit of courage.
>
> He was afraid that people would find out that he's Jewish and would betray him as a Jew to the Germans. So, the mayor was sitting next

to him and talking like as friends, you know, so that they wouldn't suspect that he might be a Jew. And he came back to Warsaw. Later, when we talked about how he survived, he would open his mouth, and we knew that he would start screaming. We had to be so quiet because the owner told everybody, all his tenants in this house, that one of the tenants left Warsaw and left all his belongings and valuables with him and he locked them up in the bathroom. It was full of things that nobody was allowed to touch. Nobody was allowed to enter the bathroom.

Lena recalls, "We behaved so quietly that we whispered." She puts her hand over her mouth and demonstrates. "Anyway, that's why we had to write things, not to have to talk." But Adek had nightmares. "So, he had a string attached to his wrist, and the rest of us had the other ends of the strings, and when one of us would see that he was about to open his mouth to scream, we would pull it to wake him up."

In his little office, the caretaker rigged a button he could press to warn them the Germans had arrived. They would be searching for Jews, arms or forbidden literature. Lena said, "This warned us to go into our 'hiding place' because the bathroom was actually our living area. The hiding place was a pantry that was about that size. [She indicated a small space.] They took out the shelves, and they had taken out those things that could betray that there was a door to this pantry and covered the whole corridor with wallpaper, attached to the skirting. There was only enough space that we could crawl under and stand there in this pantry recess, the four of us like that, when there was an alarm. When the Germans were gone, the 'all clear' was sounded and we could come out."

However, one day, Anya, the caretaker's little girl, saw the button there and pressed it. They all ran into their hiding place. Her parents didn't know, and so the four of them were standing there all day squashed together like sardines. They were hungry; they couldn't talk, cough or sneeze. For the whole day they couldn't sit or move. Lena remembers in amazement, "I don't understand how we could survive that way all day. When they came back to bring us some food, and didn't find us in the bathroom, they found us in the pantry."

Jews outside the ghetto found it hard to stay alive. Some Jews passed for Aryans but forged papers were difficult to get, and it wasn't easy to know who they could trust. Punishment was severe. Poles found sheltering Jews would be shot, including their entire family. Rewards for turning in Jews to the Germans and desire for Jewish property were significant factors in collaboration. Despite this, many Poles helped desperate Jews out of compassion or because of their Christian faith. The Polish Gentile caretaker safely hid Lena and the others for eighteen months.

20. Lena had 2 German passports

9

Jewish Resistance and the Warsaw Ghetto Uprising

Goodbye my friend. Perhaps we will see each other again. The main thing is this: My life's dream has become a reality. I have seen the Jewish defense of the ghetto in all its strength and glory.

–Mordechai Anielewicz,
April 1943 (Yad Vashem 2018b)

Evian Conference

The Germans annexed Austria, resulting in "the integration" (*Anschluss*) on 13 March 1938. The Germans dismissed Jews from the public service, and persecuted and pressured them to leave Austria. But where could they go? Eleven days after *Anschluss*, US President Franklin D. Roosevelt invited thirty-two countries to the Evian Conference at Évian-les-Bains, France, 6–16 July 1938, to discuss the increasing Jewish refugee problem. However, most countries closed their doors or agreed to take insignificant numbers. This indifference on the part of the nations to the Jewish plight only emboldened Hitler, who disdainfully commented:

It is a shameful spectacle to see how the whole democratic world is oozing sympathy for the poor tormented Jewish people, but remains hard-hearted and obdurate when it comes to helping them. (Blakeney 1985)

Most nations cited economic reasons for not taking Jewish refugees. The Australian delegate, Lieutenant Colonel Thomas White, as the Minister for Trade and Customs, used race as a reason and the nutshell of his comment is on display at Yad Vashem for all the world to see. He said, "As we have no real racial problem, we are not desirous of importing one..." (Miller 2012). When I asked a guide at Yad Vashem on one of my visits why they had singled out Australia when other countries had also closed their doors, she told me they considered that other nations thought the same as Australia but Australia was more honest.

An extract of White's speech can shed some more light on Australia's attitude:

Nevertheless, the Government of the Commonwealth of Australia has had very much in mind the problem of foreign migration as well, and a proportion of new arrivals during recent years have been from foreign sources. Realising the unhappy plight of German and Austrian Jews, they have been included on a pro rata basis which we venture to think is comparable with that of any other country. To ensure that the new arrivals are suitable, they are very largely sponsored by the Australian Jewish Welfare Society.

Under the circumstances, Australia cannot do more, for it will be appreciated that in a young country man power from the source from which most of its citizens have sprung is preferred, while undue privileges cannot be given to one particular class of non-British subjects without injustice to others. It will no doubt be appreciated also that, as we have no real racial problem, we are not desirous of importing one by encouraging any scheme of large-scale foreign migration.

Moreover, it will, I hope, be also realised that, in the particular circumstances of our development, we are confining migration principally to those who will engage in trades and occupations in which there is opportunity for work without detriment to the employment of our own people." (Miller 2012)

Kristallnacht

Jewish life in Germany and Austria was shattered on 9–10 November 1938 in what is called *Kristallnacht*, or the Night of the Broken Glass, because of the shards of glass from the windows of Jewish businesses, synagogues and homes that were smashed in the anti-Jewish pogrom. Adolph Hitler and Joseph Goebbels ordered it as a reprisal for the death of Ernst vom Rath, a German diplomat, who was shot in Paris by a Polish Jew. Goebbels stirred up the stormtroopers. Gestapo chief Heinrich Müller sent telegrams to police throughout the nation not to arrest the perpetrators but to arrest the victims, and fire stations were ordered not to put out the fires on Jewish properties.

More than 1000 synagogues were burned or damaged, and 7500 Jewish businesses were ransacked, along with schools, hospitals and cemeteries. The Germans killed 91 Jews and arrested 30,000 Jewish men. The rioters caused damage amounting to millions of reichsmarks and, incredibly, the Jewish people collectively were fined one billion reichsmarks for damage to their own property. The Nazis also confiscated their insurance claim money.

After the horror of *Kristallnacht*, Australia decided to take another 15,000 refugees, including Jews. Only 7000–8000 Jews had made it to Australia before World War Two broke out. After the war, Australia became one of the highest receiving nations per capita of Jewish refugees. But it was too late for many.

As Foreign Minister, Kevin Rudd apologised to Yad Vashem in December 2010. The occasion was when Rudd made a speech honouring William Cooper when Yad Vashem named a Chair of Resistance to the Holocaust after him. The next day Rudd apologised to the government of Israel at a meeting at King David hotel. (Miller 2012)

This apology followed a ten-year campaign by our Centre for International Reconciliation and Peace (Miller 2012) and lobbying by some Christian groups, who hoped that their nation's apology would stand next to the sign about their Evian failure. For the seventieth anniversary of Israel as a modern state, the Australian parliament passed a bipartisan motion of congratulations, as well as an apology regarding Evian.

The Jewish News records it:

> The world "turned its back on God's chosen people", federal MP Stuart Robert said last week while moving a parliamentary motion apologising for Australia's "indifference" to the plight of European Jewry on the eve of the Holocaust.
>
> During the 1938 Evian Conference, Australian representative Lieutenant Colonel T. W. White declared that while the fate of Europe's Jews was of "urgent importance", Australia "cannot do more" to assist.
>
> Speaking to a motion he moved to "make right a great wrong", and congratulate Israel on its 70th year of independence, Robert – the Liberal member for Fadden – said the indifference shown by Australia almost 80 years ago "worsened the impact of the Holocaust..."
>
> He added, "As we do this, I request that this motion be presented to Yad Vashem in this 70th year, asking that the apology be displayed beside

Lieutenant Colonel White's statement of 1938."
(Narunksy 2018)

Refugees from Germany on SS *St Louis*

Over 900 Jews fled persecution in Germany on a luxury cruise liner, the SS *St Louis*. With Cuban visas, they hoped to go to Cuba and later the USA. However, the Cuban authorities withdrew most visas as they tried to land, and they were turned away in Havana. They sailed towards Florida but were rejected by the USA as well. The German captain tried in vain to find them refuge. The liner had no choice but to return to Europe. The heartbroken Jews knew their future was uncertain and they might face death. They feared that nobody wanted them.

With Germany's borders closed by early 1939 and many countries instituting quotas on the number of Jewish refugees, the situation was dire. Fortunately, Belgium, France, Holland, and the UK agreed to take the refugees, so they did not have to go back to Nazi Germany. The American Jewish Joint Distribution Committee (JDC) came to the rescue by posting a substantial cash guarantee as part of an arrangement to cover costs. Despite this, more than 250 of them were killed by the Nazis as they overran Europe. (Lanchin 2014)

Why didn't the Jews resist?

Some people ask, "Why didn't the Jews resist? Why did they go like lambs to the slaughter?" However, it is a myth that the Jews did not resist. As famous Holocaust survivor, author and Nobel Prize-winning advocate for peace and human rights Elie Wiesel said, "The question is not why the Jews did not fight but how so many did! Tortured, starved, forced into hard labor...how did they find the strength to resist?" (Zuckerman 2013)

They resisted in ghettos, concentration camps and labour camps, by joining with partisan movements and by fighting with the Allied forces as part of the regular army. After the war, squads hunted down and killed known Nazi murderers who had gone into hiding to evade justice.

But how do we define resistance? Martin Gilbert has a broad take on it. He says:

> Even passivity was a form of resistance. To die with dignity was a form of resistance. To resist the demoralizing, brutalizing force of evil, to refuse to be reduced to the level of animals, to live through the torment, to outlive the tormentors, these too were acts of resistance. Merely to give witness of these events in testimony was, in the end, a contribution to victory. Simply to survive was a victory of the human spirit. (Gilbert 1986)

For Lena to survive to tell her story to thousands of adults and children in Australia face to face and to children in Warsaw by Skype is resistance. For her to write her diary and be interviewed for this book and some newspaper articles is resistance. Lena also actively helped the resistance in the ghetto before she escaped.

Yad Vashem identifies the spiritual resistance that occurred in the ghetto (Yad Vashem 2018d). Despite the deliberate policies of dehumanisation of Jewish people and challenges to their faith from such demoralising treatment, they kept their religious, cultural and social practices as much as they could. Maintaining their human dignity, their compassion to others and their strong moral code was important. This had enabled their community to survive not only centuries but thousands of years of violent oppression, and to keep their identity.

Over centuries, despite slavery in Egypt, the deportation of the northern tribes of Israel to Assyria, the capture of the southern tribes in Babylon and near annihilation in the time of Haman and the Medo-Persian empire, the Jews have survived. Despite the oppression of the Romans, the crusades, the pogroms, the Spanish and

Portuguese Inquisitions, the banning of Jews from England and other nations and the Holocaust, the Jews have survived and flourished.

Despite the horror of daily facing death, Jews in the ghettos organised schools, hospitals, orphanages and soup kitchens. Adults read religious texts and had prayer meetings. They observed the Sabbath and biblical feasts. Some ghettos put on concerts and theatre events, and people wrote poetry, made art and produced newspapers. Some wondered if this was frivolous, but it helped to give people the will to survive, and to maintain dignity and identity. Even the children who risked their lives to smuggle food into the ghetto were resisters against the rules of the Germans.

There were obstacles to armed resistance, however. The Germans ruled by terror and they had superior arms – tanks, cannons, machine guns – and were a trained military force, whereas the Jews in the ghetto, as well as starving and in poor health, had only a few revolvers they managed to smuggle in, and were untrained. The Germans also used deception by telling people being deported from the ghetto that they were being resettled in labour camps in the east. They offered the starving Jews quantities of bread and jam to go, so some volunteered.

Others were rounded up, mercilessly being killed on the spot if they refused. The Germans even disguised staging posts to look like regular train stations and the gas chambers to look like showers. The Germans squashed them into locked freight trains at the *Umschlagplatz* – a train station at the northern border of the ghetto – for the horrifying journey to Treblinka. However, some of those who had been assigned to look after the clothes of the deceased managed to escape from Treblinka death camp and made it back to the Warsaw ghetto to warn the others. Still, there was a lot of scepticism that the Germans could be slaughtering Jews on such a mass scale. This level of this inhumanity was difficult to imagine or believe.

In 1492, on 9 Av on the Hebrew calendar, Spain banished all Jews. Is it a coincidence that in 1942, the 9 Av fell on 22 July, the day of the great deportation from the Warsaw Ghetto? The Jews would have been well aware of the significance of this date, as 9 Av (*Tisha B'Av*) is a day marked by fasting and sorrow each year because it has been a day of destruction for Jewish people. Both Holy Temples in Jerusalem were destroyed on 9 Av, the First Temple in 423 BCE by the Babylonians, and the Second Temple in 70 CE by the Romans. The *Bar Kochba* revolt against the Romans was defeated, with the Jews of Betar killed on 9 Av 135 CE. The Temple Mount, Judaism's holiest site, was ploughed over by the Romans on the following 9 Av. In 1290, England expelled all its Jews on 9 Av.

Some Jewish teachers go further and add both world wars to this list:

> World War II and the Holocaust, historians conclude, was actually the long-drawn-out conclusion of World War I that began in 1914. And yes, amazingly enough, Germany declared war on Russia, effectively catapulting the First World War into motion, on the 9th of Av, *Tisha b'Av*.
>
> What do you make of all this? Jews see this as another confirmation of the deeply held conviction that history isn't haphazard; events – even terrible ones – are part of a Divine plan and have spiritual meaning. The message of time is that everything has a rational purpose, even though we don't understand it. (Chabad.org 2018)

It is indeed difficult to understand, and there does seem to be a pattern when we take into account the massive destruction of the Holocaust on this sad anniversary of other catastrophic events.

Warsaw Ghetto Uprising

The Jewish Fighting Organisation *(Zydowska Organizacja Bojowa*, or ZOB) was formed in response to these terrifying developments, with Mordechai Anielewicz becoming the leader. Another resistance movement, the Jewish Military Union (*Zydowski Związek Wojskowy*, or ZZW), was founded by the *Betar* movement and commanded by Pawel Frenkel. They made ghetto residents aware of the murderous purpose of Treblinka and called on them to prepare for an armed uprising by building bunkers and making homemade weapons.

The second expulsion, 18 January 1943

ZOB planned to have a demonstration in the ghetto on 21 January and arrest Jewish police. Placards were posted encouraging Jews not to go like sheep to slaughter and not to go to the train. ZOB was encouraging those who couldn't fight to act in passive resistance by hiding and not cooperating. But the Germans arrived first.

On 18 January, motorcycles and trucks burst into the ghetto with armed Germans and Ukrainians. They shouted at Jews to get out into the streets and assemble. This time they refused. The soldiers brutally hauled out resisters and fired on them, Germans too. Even some members of the *Judenrat* and their families were taken. Jews hid in attics and cellars, and behind false walls, with the Germans trying to ferret them out. The expulsion lasted until 23 January.

Anielewicz's battle plan was basic but effective – 12 fighters would join the line going to the *Umschlagplatz* and then, on signal, would break out of the lines and fire on the Germans. The Jews only had pistols compared with the semi-automatic weapons of the Germans but, with the element of surprise, they executed their plan. Germans were shot and many Jews escaped with their lives. The Germans were shocked, not expecting any resistance, let alone armed resistance. Some Germans were killed, some were wounded and some ran, leaving their weapons for ZOB to collect. The Germans set fire to Anielewicz's residence but he escaped.

Another ZOB group, under Zuckerman, opened fire when Germans invaded their home. Two Germans were wounded and one Jew died. Still another group resisted. Things changed that day. The Germans no longer searched attics and cellars with impunity. The sense of hopelessness among the Jews gave way to defiance.

The January resistance made the April rebellion possible because Jews saw they could escape and Germans could be killed. The total hopelessness disappeared. The ZOB had appeared openly in the streets and prevented Jews being taken to their death, so this made the people warm to them.

Nevertheless, 200 German SS and 800 auxiliaries from Ukraine and the Baltic states deported or killed 5000 to 6500 Jews, a heavy toll. On the last day, the Germans killed 1000 Jews in a mass slaughter in retaliation for Jewish resistance.

Despite this, the Jews no longer saw ZOB as being a danger to their survival by stirring up German retaliation. The Jews now saw them as saviours.

Jews and Poles thought the ghetto was to be completely emptied and the Jews thought they had stopped the deportations after four days. Himmler ordered the total annihilation of the ghetto and erasing of the Jews on 16 February. But it appears that in the January deportations the Germans were only reducing the number of Jews.

Himmler wanted 16,000 Jewish workers, equipment and materials transported to Lublin before the ghetto was destroyed. There was tension in the German leadership over getting rid of the Jews and keeping enough workers for the war effort, making munitions, uniforms and shoes.

Many workshops were privately owned by Germans, such as Töebbens, which made its fortunes from Jewish labour. ZOB managed to save some from being transported and many workers refused to turn up for relocation. Nevertheless, the Germans focused on moving factories, equipment and workers out of the ghetto while the ZOB prepared.

Over 600 bunkers were built to withstand the inevitable German onslaughts. The better bunkers were well planned, linked to the water and electricity supply of the city and had bunk beds, sanitary arrangements, long-life food, medicines, a camouflaged source of air and a concealed entrance.

While unity had been a problem before, now twenty-two fighting groups of the youth movement unified under ZOB while operating independently – Dror had five groups, Hashhomer Hatzair and the *Bund* and Communists had four groups each. The following had one group each – Gordonia, Akiva, Honoar Hazioni, Left Po'alei Zion and Po'alei Zion C.S. There were close relationships within and between the groups.

The ghetto was divided into the central area, the workshop area and the brushmakers area, with the overall commander being Anielewicz. Israel Kanal commanded nine groups, which were dispersed, the workshop area had eight squads commanded by Zuckerman and the brushmakers had five squads commanded by Marek Edelman.

Jacob Lejkin, who acted as police commander during the expulsion and feverishly carried out German orders, was killed by ZOB on 29 October. Soon after, they killed Yisrael First. He was an employee of the *Judenrat* and was a confidant of the German police. These executions sent a strong warning sign to others. In total, they shot thirteen collaborators over a period. While they maintained secrecy, ZOB became the real rulers of the ghetto, not the *Judenrat*.

As ZOB had no fighting experience and few weapons, they could not fight street to street because their pistols were short range, so they relied on another strategy. They planned to fight from rooftops and then disappear in a labyrinth of attics and hidden passages. They formed passages between the roofs, passages using ladders. ZOB could have had an escape plan, such as tunnelling out to the Aryan side or even building bunkers. However, they planned to die fighting. On 19 April 1943, the Eve of Passover, the Nazis attacked.

Lookouts posted on rooftops warned the people on 18 April that troops had surrounded the ghetto. There were rumours that the Germans planned to liquidate the ghetto. People took their food, medicine and bedding to their bunkers. The network of bunkers and tunnels was like an underground Jewish city. But how safe were they?

About 750 ZOB and 250 ZZW fighters were ready to face the Germans and their henchmen. Amazingly, they faced an average of over 2000 German soldiers each day (including SS, regular army and police). The Germans had large numbers of rifles and machine guns, and some tanks. They also had three armoured cars, a cannon and a flamethrower. The Jews had pistols, hand grenades and homemade Molotov cocktails. Jewish police did not take part in the first attack. The Germans used some as hostages or shields.

At 4 am, the Germans attacked and Jews counterattacked, to the shock of Germans, some Germans falling. The tank burst into flames and twelve Germans died. After a half-hour battle, the Germans withdrew. "The Jews have arms!" was the cry. The Germans slaughtered most of the Jewish fighters who took part in this battle. A Jewish blue and white flag and the Polish flag flew in triumph and defiance from the roof of a ZZW house.

Shockwaves went through the German command. The Germans considered this a political and military defeat and they replaced the officer in charge, Colonel Von Sammern. SS General Stroop, his replacement, attacked the ghetto a few hours later. The 580 Jews captured on the first day were killed on the spot because this was too few for a transport.

The Germans had a habit of attacking on Jewish (biblical) festivals or holy days. It was Passover eve (*Erev Pesach*) 1943, and the Jews managed somehow to make their kitchens *kosher*, make *matzot*, or unleavened bread, and to find some wine for the occasion. Facing death, they still wanted to obey God's commands and observe their religion and customs. Secular Jews followed the traditions of their forefathers. Shoshana Baharir, a Warsaw ghetto survivor, gave a moving account:

> It was Passover eve, 1943, and we had arranged everything in the house in preparation for the holiday. We even had *Matzot*, everything. We had made the beds... The policeman who lived with us always told us everything that was going to happen... He told us, "You should know that the ghetto is surrounded – with Ukrainians. Tonight will not be a good night." He had heard this. We took all our belongings and went into the bunker. Why wait?... So, we took what we still had at home, whatever food

81

we had, everything, and went down into the bunker. And waited. (Yad Vashem 2018e)

The Germans entered the ghetto and met fierce resistance, as the Jewish fighters knew the Germans planned to kill them anyway. But the Passover *Seder* continued in probably more than one bunker. While Tuvia Borzykowski was a member of ZOB, she wanted to observe Passover. Here is her account, probably white tablecloth and all, the incongruity of it lit large:

> Amidst this destruction, the table in the center of the room looked incongruous with glasses filled with wine, with the family seated around, the rabbi reading the *Haggadah*. His reading was punctuated by explosions and the rattling of machine-guns; the faces of the family around the table were lit by the red light from the burning buildings nearby. (Borzykowski 1976)

Passover is a story of how G-D (God) brought the Hebrews out of Egypt, where they were slaves to the Egyptians. How ironic that in German-occupied Europe they were slaves of the Germans, doing forced labour in the ghettos, concentration camps or labour camps. For those who survived, their liberation was still to come.

Hitler's fifty-fourth birthday was on 20 April. The Germans attacked the home where flags had been raised and ZZW commander Leon Rodal was killed. Polish police were assisting Germans in the ghetto warfare and ZOB wished the Polish underground could supply them better with arms.

Yitzhak Zuckerman was ZOB's representative to Armia Krajowa (AK) and Henryk Wolinski was the representative on AK for the Jews. The Germans and Poles were both worried the uprising would spread out of the ghetto to Warsaw but AK wanted to hold back its fighting force until the Germans and Soviets had exhausted each other.

After three or four days, the Germans set fires sporadically and then systematically to destroy the ghetto and nests of resisters. Some Jews hid in sewage canals, which enabled them to move between bunkers or get to the Aryan side, although it wasn't easy to find their way out.

In another ploy, the Germans "caught" 5200 Jews who had assembled in the munitions workshop after being told they could survive by being transferred to another work camp outside the ghetto – Poniatowa. However, by November 1943 the Jews taken to work camps in Poniatowa and Trawniki were murdered.

The Warsaw Ghetto became the centre of a Jewish–German war – "the third front". Twenty tanks were seen going to the ghetto. The Germans cut off the water supply and electricity, worsening the siege-like conditions. However, there were some wells in the ghetto area.

Although the fighters rescued hundreds of Jews destined for transportation, there were still many they could not save. On 25 April, the Germans captured 1690 Jews and shot 270, with hundreds more buried in blown-up bunkers or burned in the flames.

On 25 April it was Easter and a carousel operated just over the ghetto wall with people holidaymaking, laughing and riding high, despite the smoke and the smell of burning. Some of the Jews in the ghetto could not understand why life was going on as usual on the Aryan side, or the Christian quarter, just over the wall. One inmate of the ghetto looked from the roof of his dwelling and saw the amusement park filled with people taking their children on an outing. "How could they? Didn't they know what was happening to us? Didn't they care?"

The "bunker wars" went on for a month, with the Germans systematically burning and exploding buildings. Some Jews were burnt alive in the bunkers, and high numbers, including children, jumped from burning buildings or used bedsheets to get out. The Germans shot those who survived. A few managed to escape to the Aryan side and join the Polish partisans in their fight against the Germans. Burnt buildings were falling on top of bunkers, burying the people. The

Germans used dogs and listening devices to locate those still hiding and lobbed poisonous gases into the bunkers.

As the Germans burnt the buildings to the ground, the inside of the bunkers, which had brick and concrete, became furnace-like and it was almost impossible to breathe. The heat increased by the hour. Men and women removed most of their clothes to try to cope. Nervous tension gripped them, as well as the fear of discovery.

Fighting was still occurring in the streets. An occasional Molotov cocktail and a few revolver shots from Jewish fighters rang out, and machine gun fire and powerful explosions rocked the air from German positions. The scene was devastating as people ran from bunker to bunker knocking frantically on buildings still standing, hoping for shelter. Damaged piping, charred wood, broken glass, window frames, tin, piles of bricks and scattered household belongings littered the streets.

One survivor described the hellish scene:

> The fire causes a huge commotion on the street. People with bundles run from house to house, from street to street, there is no rescue, no one knows where to take shelter. They seek desperately, nothing, no rescue, no protection, death prevails everywhere. The ghetto walls are completely surrounded, no one can enter or leave. [The] clothes are burning on people's bodies. Screams of pain and crying, houses and bunkers are burning, everything, everything is in flames. (Yad Vashem 2018c)

Israel Gutman writes: "The entire ghetto was ablaze. Thousands of people near physical and mental collapse – virtually on the verge of madness – not only maintained this way of life but viewed its disappearance as a great catastrophe." (Gutman 2012)

Jews routed out of bunkers by the Germans often fired bullets rather than giving in. The Germans used dogs and sound detectors to find them and coerced informants with promises of clemency to reveal other bunker entrances. Even after the entrances to bunkers were blown up, some refused to leave and asphyxiating gas was used. Bunkers became "burning cages" without food, water or air. Sometimes the people could only crawl out of the bunkers, exhausted.

Despite regular sympathetic updates in their Polish underground newsletters of the massacres of Jews in the ghetto, and despite a request from the Polish government in exile in Britain to assist them, Britain gave none. The Jews were alone. Most Poles watched the fires and smoke from the ghetto and heard the thunder of bombs and explosives destroying it, and kept silent, did nothing.

The Germans were still managing to transport Jews. On 1 May, the Germans bombed the sewage canals and sealed the entrances, and some Jews who had escaped were caught and shot.

On 3 May, the Germans attacked a bunker on Franciszkanska Street and killed half the ZOB fighters, some escaping to 18 Mila Street. A group of criminals had a well-supplied bunker there and took them in. Three hundred people, including 120 Jewish fighters, were in what has become known as "Mila 18" and it became the centre of the uprising. Shmuel Asher was in charge of the criminal underworld and they had electricity, a well and food smuggled from Warsaw via the sewers.

Mila 18 captured, 8 May

Commander Stroop reports capturing the bunker on 8 May and executing the leaders of the Warsaw Ghetto Uprising. However, Gutman writes that Vladka Meed, a courier for ZOB, wrote in her memoirs of the end of the command post at Mila 18. (Gutman 2012)

> The Germans surrounded it on May 8. They demanded the Jews come out, and the owners of the bunker did, but the fighters refused with weapons ready to fight. The Germans poured in poison gas and threw explosives. Suffocating,

some of the fighters managed to escape but the
decision was taken to take their lives rather than
surrender to the Germans. It was a sad end to a
heroic resistance.

Anielewicz's body was never found but is believed to be in the
ruins of the bunker where he died with his girlfriend Mira Fuchrer.
Many women fighters used guns and many women were couriers,
smuggling food, weapons, medicine, documents and people through
the sewers. Marek Edelman, one of few surviving commanders, managed to escape the attack on Mila 18 that day, through the sewers.
Of those who fled Mila 18, seven suffered poisoning, including Tosia
Altman and did not live after all.

However, the resistance didn't stop. There were still bunkers with
Jews returning fire.

ZZW fighters had planned to fight and then escape from the
ghetto but as their contacts on the Polish side were poor, few survived.
It was also very challenging to find a way through the sewers to the
Aryan side and couriers who knew the way were needed. There was
a successful escape by some ZOB fighters and bunker dwellers on 30
April, led by a courier who was killed when she went back to guide
more through. The Germans also laid siege to some ZOB survivors
and families in the tunnels and they perished.

The fighting continued for twenty-eight days with an incredible
show of bravery from those with so few weapons to defend themselves. Most perished in the fires, and the Nazis sent the remainder
to Treblinka, Madjanek and Lublin camps. On 16 May, the Germans
proclaimed their victory over the Jews of Warsaw by destroying the
Great Synagogue on Tlomackie Street. Jurgen Stroop, the commander
of the SS unit that suppressed the uprising, was determined to destroy
the Jewish quarter of Warsaw.

Stroop called the Jews bandits and he reported to Krüger, the
head of the HSSPF (Higher SS and Police Leader) and police, that of
the 56,065 Jews who were caught, 7000 were wiped out on the spot

in the great action, 6929 were wiped out in Treblinka and they killed 5000 to 6000 in bombing and fires. (Gutman 2012)

Between 15,000 and 20,000 Jews went into hiding after the uprising and lived on borrowed or fictitious papers with the help of the Poles. It is not known how many of these survived but, in the Polish uprising, a group of Jews, some of them from ZOB, fought under Zuckerman. Little information went out to the free press and none to the German media.

The image of Jews was no longer one of a passive people, but one of young warriors who met an honourable death. It was not Jewish passivity that drove the final solution but Nazi depravity, as their rage heightened with Jewish resistance.

Greek and other non-Slavic-speaking Jews were brought in by the Nazis as forced labour to clean up the ghetto amid the stench of burnt flesh. The cleaned red bricks were daily picked up to be reused by the Germans, as was so much Jewish wealth stolen from Jews in ghettos and concentration camps.

The Warsaw Ghetto Uprising was the largest single uprising by Jews in World War Two, and it inspired others to rise up. Uprisings followed in the Auschwitz, Treblinka and Sobibor death camps and in the Czestochowa, Bialystok, Vilna, Tuczyn and Minsk ghettos.

There were about 750 active fighters, mostly young men and women. Few survived. Lena's brother Salek was one who did not, and Lena came close to being one of them too. But her fate was to be different. She was to live to tell the story. Pawel Frenkel, commander of ZZW was also killed in action, possibly on the Aryan side. In the early days of the fighting, Anielewicz, whose nickname was "Aniolek" or "Little Angel", wrote:

> What happened exceeded our boldest dreams. The Germans fled twice from the ghetto. One of our companies held its position for forty minutes, while the other one lasted upwards of six hours... I cannot describe to you the conditions in which the Jews are living. Only a hand-

ful will survive. All the rest will succumb, sooner or later. Their fate has been sealed. In almost all of the bunkers in which our friends are hiding one cannot even light a candle at night, for lack of air… Goodbye my friend. Perhaps we will see each other again. The main thing is this: My life's dream has become a reality. I have seen the Jewish defense of the ghetto in all its strength and glory. (Jewish Virtual Library 2018b)

After liberation, the streets of the ghetto were unrecognisable but they found the ruins of Mila 18 and erected a black stone as a memorial to Anieleweiz and the ZOB. An impressive memorial to the fighters has been built, and every anniversary, on 19 April, Mark Edelman, the last surviving commander of the uprising, laid daffodils there until his death in 2009.

A tiny enclave of the Warsaw ghetto survives today. There are blocks of stories-high, brown brick flats with white window frames. Condemned buildings have windows that don't close properly, broken bricks and crumbling walls. Windows lower down are boarded up with grey slats. Grey brick paths with a few tufts of green grass lead the way to these buildings where dreams died, hopes faded, but the Jews showed remarkable resilience. Despite the deliberate dehumanisation of the Jews by the Germans, the Jews did not put their own needs above others, but there was caring, sharing and bravery.

Simcha Rotem, the last surviving fighter of the Warsaw Ghetto Uprising, passed away at the age of 94 in December 2018. Rotem served as a courier helping fighters to escape from the ghetto. His Polish nickname was Kazik.

21. Evian Conference Delegates 1938, Yad Vashem Archives 4613-425

22. Susanna Kokkonen and Shaya Ben Yehuda, left, receiving plaque of apology re Australia's position at Evian from Norman and Barbara Miller 2010

23. Madeburg, Germany People Looking at Ruined Businesses
after Kristallnacht, Yad Vashem Archives 135GO7

24. Baden, Germany Arrest of Jews on Kristallnacht,
Yad Vashem Archives 138FO8

25. Warsaw, Poland, 1943, Waffen SS Soldiers Beside a
Burning Building during the Warsaw Ghetto Uprising,
Yad Vashem Archives, Jerusalem 4613/733

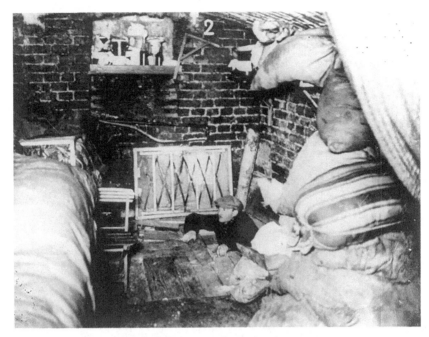

26. Warsaw Ghetto Bunker

27. Jews Pulled from a Bunker, Stroop Report, Warsaw Ghetto Uprising

28. German Stormtroopers Force Warsaw Ghetto Dwellers
to Evacuate Their Homes, Yad Vashem Archives 359/76

29. Warsaw Ghetto Uprising, Jews Deported, photo Stroop Report

30. Warsaw Ghetto Uprising, Jews Lined Up Against the Wall

31. Warsaw Ghetto Uprising Memorial Rear

10

Treblinka Uprising

The only real heroes, I guess, were those (almost all of them had lost their wives and children in Treblinka) who remained and, clearly purposely, enabled the others to escape, 'so that at least someone might possibly live to bear witness'.

—Richard Glazar, a survivor of Treblinka

In December 1941, on the outskirts of Moscow, Hitler's war in Europe was lost, although it dragged on for a few more years. It was no longer winnable. When the Germans invaded Russia in June 1941, they were victorious. But Russia is large and the Germans failed to advance quickly enough before the winter, Hitler being diverted by wanting to take Ukraine. In –35C temperatures, lacking warm clothing and brought almost to a standstill, the German army was too exhausted to continue to Moscow. On 6 December 1941, Russia counterattacked the exhausted Germans with fresh reinforcements from Siberia and the Russian far east The Germans were defeated for the first time. The next day, Japan bombed Pearl Harbour, and the USA entered the war. These two events were turning points in World War Two.

German assurances of winning the war were slipping away when Reichsführer-SS Heinrich Himmler visited Treblinka in February 1943 and ordered that all evidence of the mass executions be destroyed. Also relevant was that there were few Polish Jews left to exterminate, so their work was winding up. The bodies of 60,000 to 70,000 people who they had gassed were dug up and burned on pyres with the ashes reburied in the original pits. It was a massive cover-up and heartrending work for the Jewish slave workers who had to do all the dirty work for the Germans.

When the decomposing corpses were dug up, large amounts of money and other valuables were found in the stomachs of those victims who had been hoping this would help them start a new life. Of course, the plunder was retrieved for the German coffers, hungry for as much blood money as they could get. What was robbing the dead to them? They had already robbed these innocents of life.

Many of the Jewish death brigade vomited at the smell of the decomposing bodies. The odour of death that filled the air was nauseating. The Jewish workers, forced to do this, couldn't stomach it longer than a few weeks and were replaced by other teams. Treblinka survivor Hershl Sperling, who wrote an account of his time in Treblinka described it: "Even the SS units are changed every two weeks, and sent on immediate leave; even the murderers themselves cannot bear this diabolical bestiality." (Smith 2010)

Sperling says he only once met an SS man in Treblinka who would not participate in this inhumanity. That officer found everything so unbelievable that he pulled a Jew aside and asked him to tell him the truth.

"'Impossible, impossible!' He kept murmuring, shaking his head slowly as he spoke. From that day on he was never seen again" (Smith 2010). Whether he was killed by the SS or sent to the front to die, is not known.

The gruesome work continued till the thousands of bodies were dug up and burned. It took a huge emotional toll on the slave labourers. Was this the tipping point or was it the news of the Warsaw Ghetto Uprising that spurred the Treblinka Uprising? In the early days of Treblinka, Jews used to try to escape almost daily but then the controls tightened and the reaction of the Germans was vicious. Runaways were invariably caught and hung by their feet on a high pole till they died in excruciating pain. This was done publicly to strike fear into the others, who still wanted to cling to life, even in this hellhole.

However, they were not deterred. They buried some money and valuables, reserved from the plunder of dead Jews, as they knew they would need money to be able to survive once they escaped. They could exchange it for food, and maybe even shelter, from the Polish farmers living in the woods nearby. Tension rose when a Jewish *Kapo* or supervisor was searched, found to have a sack of gold and shot on the spot.

Sperling, whose account of Treblinka and the uprising was written about a year after the war, described it:

> Engineer Galewski, *Lagerältester*, the new *Kapo* Kurland, and Moniek, of the 'yard-Jews' were the leaders of the uprising. A fourteen-year-old Jewish boy steals into the Ukrainian guardroom at night, removes weapons, bullets and several machine-guns. The arms are divided out, and the day on which the revolt will be launched is decided upon. (Smith 2010)

On that day, Commandant Franz and forty Ukrainians were due to leave the camp to bathe in the Bug River. The signal was to be a shot, which was planned for 6 am. However, the plan was threatened by the arrest of twenty Jews found in possession of gold. This was a sign to the SS of an intended escape. As they were marching the Jews off to the *Lazarett* to kill them, the ringleaders decided to launch the revolt straight away by throwing a hand grenade at Franz. Sperling's eyewitness account shows the frenzy of the moment:

> The signal to fight is given and the Ukrainian SS open heavy fire on the Jews. But the Jews remain firm, throw hand grenades and position their machine-guns. Some Ukrainians fall, and the thousand or so Jews in the camp break through the fence. (Smith 2010)

They escaped into the woods under heavy fire, which felled some. Other escapees managed to cut telephone lines and disable vehicles. They lit petrol and set Treblinka on fire. Flames burst skyward as the death camp went up in flames and the SS, shocked, began to shoot indiscriminately.

However, soon the chase was on. The Jews broke into small groups in the hope that some would not be caught. Panting, starved and exhausted, the escapees ran for their lives. Wracked with hunger, tormented by the fear of capture, they pushed themselves onward. They hid by day and travelled by night. The will to survive pushed them on, although it would have been so easy to give up. Sperling and his two friends managed to find Polish peasants who fed them and gave them more food for their journey. They could not stay there, however, as the SS were searching all the villages. Eventually, they managed to exchange a diamond ring for Polish money and caught the train to Warsaw, continuously fearful of being discovered.

Sperling's friend and mentor, Shmuel Rajzman, survived with him. However, most of the escapees were soon captured and killed in that frightening chase. He estimated only twenty survived.

The uprising took place on 2 August 1943. Steiner wrote a novel on Treblinka after interviewing survivors and his story, which is a fictionalised account, differs from Sperling's:

> All the members of the Committee and most of those who played a role in the uprising of the camp died in the revolt. Of the thousand prisoners who were in the camp at the time, about six hundred managed to get out and to reach the nearby forests without being recaptured.
>
> Of these six hundred escapees, there remained, on the arrival of the Red Army a year later, only forty survivors. The others had been killed in the course of that year by Polish peasants, partisans of the *Armia Krajowa*, Ukrainian fascist bands, deserters from the Wehrmacht, the

Gestapo and special units of the German army.
(Steiner 1994)

Other accounts say those who escaped perished from starvation or exposure to freezing conditions or were recaptured.

One of the survivors, Richard Glazar, who describes the Jewish prisoners as more dead-than-alive slaves and gravediggers, disputes the accuracy of Steiner's account of the Treblinka Uprising. He says:

> Naturally, in the first moments, it was as joyful as you make it out, something which nothing and nobody could hold back; grenades and bottles of petrol were exploding, guns taken from Ukrainian guards were being fired, and then the petrol tank blew up. After that there was utter confusion – you should have seen us the way we all got tangled up, how we knew not where and in which direction to go, and they were firing to us. Then Lublink, the orderly, ran up and drove one group in front of him to escape, he had only some sort of cane in his hand, and he swished it about in front of him as though he were driving a flock of geese. (Romanov 2006)

In the excitement, confusion and chaos, there are accounts of people climbing over the dead bodies of those shot trying to escape and clambering over the fence. Glazer continues, recalling the impossible odds they were dealing with and the few who survived:

> No one got as far as the guard towers standing right out in the outer field; it was senseless anyway. Look here, so few people survived, no one – possibly not even the SS – can really say what actually happened in those moments in the various parts of the camp… It would be easy for

me to leave it at that, pass on, hold my peace, and we from *Tarnung [camouflage unit]*, would emerge from your book as special heroes, who shot their way right through to the woods; yet of those, only four of us are alive today – perhaps one in Belgium, one in Poland, one in the U.S.A. and one in Czechoslovakia. And in reality? Of the twenty-five strong *Tarnung Kommando* perhaps six, possibly eight of us got to the end of the outer field and across the barbed wire fence with its anti-tank barricades. (Romanov 2006)

Accounts of the number who escaped and the number of survivors vary. One report is that several Nazis died, 200 prisoners escaped and 100 survived the chase.

According to a BBC News report, the last of 67 survivors of Treblinka, Smuel Willenberg, died in Israel in 2016 aged 93. He arrived in 1942, among 6000 Jews, and was assigned to labour duties, as he was a bricklayer. During the uprising, he survived by clambering over piled-up bodies as the Nazis shot prisoners near a fence during a mass breakout. He hid in the surrounding countryside before fleeing to Warsaw and joining the Polish underground. He lost his two sisters there. (BBC World News 2016)

A BBC documentary features survivor stories from Treblinka. The men had seen hellish things and were determined to get out and let others know. They were waiting for an order or sign. It was meant to be a shot. Someone threw a grenade onto petrol, which exploded and caught fire. They tried to grab weapons but ended up fighting over them as there were only two machine guns available. In the chaos of flames, smoke, explosions and gunfire, dozens managed to get over the fence and hide in the forest. There was a massive search. Kalman Taigman built a makeshift bunker and lived in it for a year while Smuel (Samuel) Willenberg escaped to Warsaw. Smuel fought with the Polish resistance and Kalman's testimony helped convict Adolph Eichmann in his 1961 trial. (Gangi 2015)

Kurt Franz, the last commandant, testified during his trial: "After the uprising in August 1943, I ran the camp single-handedly for a month; however, during that period no gassing was undertaken. It was during that period that the original camp was leveled off, and lupines [flowers] were planted." (Scrapbookpages.com 1998)

In August 1944, Russian scouts, following the train tracks to Warsaw, came across an unnerving forest clearing. Why had the forest been cleared? Why had an effort been made to erase evidence? But the earth could not or would not hide the horror, and they discovered some bones.

When the Soviet Red Army arrived, what had been Treblinka was eerily quiet, the blood-stained earth hiding the enormity of its shame and horror. Vasily Grossman, a Jewish war correspondent traveling with the Soviets, interviewed the forty he estimated survived and spoke to local farmers. He wrote an article called "The Hell of Treblinka" in November 1944, which was later quoted at the Nuremberg trials of Nazi war criminals.

Today, there are still some ruins – the machinery workshop and the kitchen for example. The food cellar, with stone walls and stone stairs leading down into it, still stands. Bison still roam and the forests and wetlands have been preserved, making it the "wild east" of Poland. There is some flat land on each side of the road, and farmers pull wagons with tractors or the occasional horse. In the village of Treblinka itself, the cottages today are dilapidated but the lace curtains in the windows indicate people still live here. A visitor describes the scene:

> As you get near the village of Treblinka, there is a line of beautiful chestnut trees alongside the road on the right. You see old men walking along the road, carrying bundles of sticks on their backs. There are farm families digging potatoes and burning the dried potato vines in the fields. Occasionally, you see a stork's nest on a roof near the chimney, or a large anthill at the edge of a

forest, surrounded by a tiny log fence for protection. There are old wooden Catholic churches
and white cottages with thatched roofs along the
road... The farther you travel down this road,
the farther you seem to go back in time. (Jewish
Virtual Library 2018c)

The approach to Treblinka today is memorialised by stone bars
symbolising railway lines. Six stone slabs tell the story, a cobbled path
winding its way through the green trees. The trees are tall and thin,
branches and leaves high off the ground. South of the replicated stone
train platform are the burial pits. Ten stones commemorate the Jewish
victims from various nations.

The memorial was set up between 1959 and 1962, and an exhibition centre at the camp opened in 2006. This became part of the
Siedlce Regional Museum.

A large granite memorial stone stands where the gas chambers
were located. It is like a tombstone and has a crack down the middle
as part of the design. It has a *menorah* on top, with the words "Never
Again", a rallying cry for Jewish people worldwide. Surrounding this
imposing structure are 1700 small stones of different shapes and sizes,
representing the towns and villages from which the victims came. The
largest is the Warsaw stone because it is estimated that 265,000 Jews
from Warsaw met their deaths at Treblinka. The stones are set into
concrete, as a symbolic cemetery. The ashes of the 700,000 to 800,000
people whose lives were tragically taken is buried underneath.

On 4 July 1946, well after the Nazi occupation, a mob of Poles
killed forty-two Jews in the central Polish city of Kielce, a devastating
blow to rebuilding relations. One of the 1700 stones represents Kielce.
This final blow of anti-Semitism led to many of the 300,000 Polish
Holocaust survivors fleeing the country. Another stone represents the
two cremation pyres. After the war, some Poles who had sheltered
Jews wanted to remain anonymous, so as not to be accused by their
neighbours as Jew lovers or to have their homes searched for loot.

Similarly, some Jews didn't go back to thank the Poles, as they felt it might put them at risk.

The only person to have an individual memorial stone is Janusz Korczak, a teacher who ran an orphanage in Warsaw, wrote children's books and did a weekly radio show for children. He refused the opportunity to escape from the Warsaw Ghetto and stayed with the 192 orphans when they were seized by the Germans, comforting them as he went to the gas chambers with them.

Using unique, ground-penetrating radar equipment, British forensic archaeologist Caroline Sturdy Colls uncovered hidden mass graves at Treblinka in January 2012. The Jewish Historical Museum in Warsaw has an image with an aerial view of Treblinka taken in September 1945, showing where Poles had dug thousands of holes searching for gold fillings among the bones of dead Jews. A black market had also taken place between the Treblinka death camp and the local Polish community, where the farmers exchanged food for Jewish possessions that could be resold at a profit.

****

Poland was a graveyard for Jews. All the death camps were in Poland, the others being Belzec, Chelmno, Sobibor, Majdanek and Auschwitz-Birkenau. The latter two were also forced labour camps, which were still in use when liberated by Russian soldiers towards the end of the war. The Germans had destroyed the rest before the Russians arrived to remove evidence of Nazi war crimes. Dachau, Buchenwald and Bergen-Belsen were not death camps but were concentration camps where terrible atrocities nevertheless occurred.

It is hard to believe that so many countries were allies of the Germans in their murderous rampage across Europe – Italy, Austria, Latvia, Lithuania, Estonia, Bulgaria, Rumania, Hungary, Croatia, Slovakia and Finland.

In the chaos of liberation, survivors experienced loneliness, outrage, trauma, shock, illness and exhaustion, and their sense of safety was so shattered that it was hard to get back to normality. The United

Nations Relief and Rehabilitation Administration (UNRRA), which helped survivors of war, was inadequate in coping with Jewish refugees because it assumed people could go back to their families and countries, but Jewish families and communities had been destroyed. Nationality labels were hard for Jews to accept when the countries they had lived in didn't want them. So, hundreds of displaced persons camps were set up in Germany for the 330,000 Jews no one wanted.

After the Holocaust, Jews and other prisoners had to learn to normalise, readapting to such basic things as sitting at a table using a knife and fork to eat from a plate, and not their fingers and a mug. In camp, if a person was dead, they could take their shoes or clothes because they didn't need them. They didn't call taking food or valuables stealing. They had to do it to survive. Now they needed to leave these habits behind.

Even in Palestine, the British Mandate allowed only 1500 survivors a month to emigrate. This policy was despite the Balfour Declaration of the British parliament on 31 October 1917, which stated that a homeland should be set up for Jews in Palestine, and the British receiving an international mandate from the League of Nations to do that after World War One.

32. Treblinka 11 barracks and petrol tank burning in prisoner uprising, 2 August 1943, Photo F Zabecki

33. Treblinka Memorial Place Poland

34. Janusz Korczak Memorial Treblinka

11

Warsaw Uprising: The Cost of Freedom

The city must completely disappear from the surface
of the earth and serve only as a transport station
for the Wehrmacht. No stone can remain standing.
Every building must be razed to its foundation.
—RFSS chief Heinrich Himmler,
17 October 1944, SS officers conference
(Witsuka and Tomaszewsk 2006)

While Lena and her companions hid in the bathroom, little did they know of the terror and bravery that was occurring in the streets of their city. The Polish underground resistance, led by the Polish Home Army (*Armia Krajowa*), tried to liberate Warsaw from German occupation in the summer of 1944. It was called the Warsaw Uprising (*Powstanie Warszawskie*), not to be confused with the Warsaw Ghetto Uprising. It was timed to coincide with the retreat of the German forces from Poland ahead of the Soviet advance. Considering 200,000 Poles, mostly civilians, were killed in the uprising, was this another miracle of survival for Lena?

The Polish government-in-exile in Britain approved of the uprising and left the timing to the combatants. It began on 1 August 1944 as part of a nationwide Operation Tempest. After five traumatic years of German occupation, the Home Army, also known as the citizen army, saw their chance to free their capital from the Germans, aid an allied victory and prevent the Soviet propaganda machine from taking the credit for liberating Warsaw and imposing its government on the city.

People carried goods on bicycles with carts in front. Others travelled in cabs (horses with a driver and buggy). Planter boxes of shrubs decorated the windowsills of the blocks of flats. The peaceful scenes belied the horror of the past five years. The resistance had hoped that there would be an allied victory, and they wanted justice and revenge on the Germans, confident that their fight would only take a couple of days because the Russians, who were on the edge of Warsaw, would come to their aid. Moscow radio kept sending messages to urge them on to rise up against the Germans.

At the German headquarters, swastikas decorated the buildings and trucks, and other vehicles were parked outside. It was heavily patrolled, and the Germans roamed the streets of Warsaw in smaller trucks and motorbikes with sidecars. They were heavily armed.

At 5 pm on 1 August, the citizen army struck. It was a heroic and tragic battle for their beloved city and the freedom they so passionately desired. The fighters were men and women, many of them teenagers and children. There were 40,000 fighters and less than one in four had weapons. As one man fell, others would pick up the gun and continue the fight. In desperation, they used stones, handmade grenades and flamethrowers fashioned from garden hoses. Children would crawl up to tanks and throw homemade grenades at them. They captured two tanks.

The Nazis used tanks, heavy artillery and cannons. At the height of the fighting, German planes flew bombing raids every forty minutes. Buildings were straffed by planes, tearing them apart, fragments scattering through the air. In some buildings, flames could be seen through every window. Pulverised buildings added powdery dust and ashes to the streets, which were full of rubble, rubbish and abandoned barrels. Explosions from grenades sent flames and smoke through the narrow streets of the city. Residents ran to escape the fire and firepower, choking on the dust, trying to find shelter in dilapidated buildings. Nowhere was safe. The screams of the injured shook the air while others shouted orders. Machine gun fire, staccato-like, rang out across the beleaguered city. Blood-covered bodies lay in the gutters with shattered limbs, shattered lives. The fighters barricaded some streets with large sacks and placed snipers in whatever tall buildings were left. The Germans blew holes out of brick walls, and the resistance picked up the bricks and used them for weapons.

Some members of the Jewish Fighting Organisation who had escaped after the Warsaw Ghetto Uprising had been suppressed joined the Polish Home Army in the Warsaw Uprising. Polish fighters liberated hundreds of Jews from Greece and Hungary imprisoned in the Gęsiówka concentration camp, who then joined them, serving in auxiliary units. Few survived the uprising. (Yad Vashem 2018a)

Where were the Russians? Why had their guns suddenly fallen silent? Where was the help from their allies, Britain and the USA? The underground radio operators were telling London what was happening daily.

Women fought with the men in street-to-street battles, in urban warfare, and were underground radio operators and underground couriers. They also baked bread and set up soup kitchens for the underground army, but food and water started to run out. As the uprising wore on, with little outside support, people were starving and malnourished and started drinking from puddles of water. A few looked for cats to eat.

When the Poles killed German soldiers, the Germans took revenge by grabbing civilians off the street, killing one hundred for every one soldier, methodically counting to one hundred and shooting them on the spot. The roads were strewn with dead bodies, some covered, some not. Young people lay there with the life drained out of them. The Nazis went into hospitals and slaughtered the sick and injured. To protect the ill and wounded, the Poles set up makeshift hospitals in tenements and moved from place to place to avoid capture.

Young lovers died in each other's arms, explosions tore babies from their mothers and buildings collapsed on the elderly, who were too slow to escape. The resistance started to lose hope, but they could not give up because their desire for freedom was strong and because they knew they would be killed anyway if they surrendered.

The role of the Soviets

The Soviet Red Army were on the outskirts of the city but had suspended combat operations by order of the Kremlin. If the Polish Home Army had triumphed, the Polish government-in-exile would have the right to resume its pre-war government in Poland. However, the Soviets favoured a post-war communist regime instead. A Polish communist regime had already been hastily set up in Lublin on 22 July 1944. The Soviets regarded the Polish uprising as anti-communist and not only didn't help the Polish but actively hindered them as the documentation shows:

> Declassified documents from Soviet archives reveal that Stalin gave instructions to cut off the Warsaw resistance from any outside help. The urgent orders issued to the Red Army troops in Poland on 23 August 1944 stipulated that the Home Army units in Soviet-controlled areas should be prevented from reaching Warsaw and helping the Uprising, their members apprehended and disarmed. Only from mid-September, under pressure from the Western Allies, the Soviets began to provide some limited assistance to the resistance. (Gibianskii and Naimark 2004)

In the single largest military effort undertaken by any European resistance movement during World War Two, the Poles fought street-to-street battles for sixty-three days, taking and losing ground, courageously fighting, with few weapons and supplies, and little outside support.

The plan to stage an uprising against the Germans a few days before the arrival of Allied forces worked in a number of European capitals, such as in Prague and Paris. Initially, the Poles extended their influence over most of central Warsaw, but the Soviets ignored Polish attempts to maintain radio contact with them and did not provide troop or air support, even though the Soviet base was five minutes' flying time away. This led to suspicions that Soviet leader Joseph Stalin wanted the Polish resistance vanquished. Winston Churchill, the British prime minister, pleaded with Stalin to help the Poles, who were Britain's allies. He not only refused to help but would not give air clearance for supply drops. Churchill sent over 200 low-level supply drops anyway, in an operation known as the Warsaw Airlift. After getting air clearance, the USA sent one high-level mass airdrop to the Polish resistance.

Heinrich Himmler's orders

German house-to-house clearances and mass evictions of entire neighbourhoods exposed Jewish Poles. Jewish fighters were very much a part of the Polish resistance, the Home Army. The Germans carried out Heinrich Himmler's orders, with police, special SS and *Wehrmacht* groups going from house to house, shooting civilians regardless of age or gender and burning their bodies with impunity. The policy was designed to crush the Poles' will to fight but it only hardened their resistance. Until mid-September, the Germans shot all captured resistance fighters on the spot but, after that, treated some of the captured Polish soldiers as POWs.

The people of Warsaw faced hunger and starvation as the fighting dragged on. It was with great relief that Polish units recaptured a brewery at Ceglana Street on 6 August. The people of Warsaw from then on lived mostly on barley from the brewery's warehouses with several thousand people organised into teams to distribute bags daily in the city centre. They were eating spit-soup (*pluj-zupa*) with the barley being ground in coffee grinders and boiled with water to make the soup.

The military set up a long-range radio transmitter in the city centre on 7 August. It was also used by the re-established Polish radio. It was the only such radio station in German-held Europe and was on the air three or four times a day, with news, patriotic content, appeals for help and music. Newspapers were still circulating.

Despite sustained diplomatic efforts by the Polish government in London for support for the Warsaw Uprising before it occurred, the Allies would not move without Soviet permission. Finally, a British mission arrived in Poland in December 1944. Stunningly, when they met with Soviet authorities, they were arrested and imprisoned. Nevertheless, the RAF, British Commonwealth Air Forces, and the Polish Air Force made night supply drops to Poland from airfields in Italy, but they could carry limited quantities.

Ground was won and lost and retaken but, as time wore on, it was clear they couldn't win with their lack of weapons. The Home Army evacuated the Old Town through the sewers, a few thousand each day for five days, under the noses of the Germans. There must have been some suspicions as the Germans dropped gas canisters and grenades down the sewers, killing many. While it was a successful evacuation, it took its toll. The resistance was exhausted and starving and had no weapons. It was like a descent into hell as they waded through rivers of excrement, often waist deep. It was crowded, those behind relentlessly pushing forward those in front. They persevered, on and on through the dark, slippery, murky waters. Screams pierced the air as people stepped on dead bodies, and people dropped from exhaustion. Some went mad while others suicided. The only way to survive was not to think about it, not to cry. The fumes caused some to be blind for a few days after coming out of the sewers.

The Germans killed about 16,000 members of the Polish resistance and badly wounded thousands of others. Also, 150,000 -200,000 Polish civilians were killed, mostly in mass executions.

Lack of help from the Soviets enabled the Germans to regroup and defeat the Polish resistance. They signed the final surrender on 2 October and the *Wehrmacht* agreed to treat Home Army soldiers in accord with the Geneva Convention, and to treat civilians humanely.

The Germans sent 15,000 resistance fighters to POW camps in Germany. Somewhere between 5000 and 6000 resistance fighters managed to blend into the civilian population. The Germans may have suspected this, and they expelled the entire civilian population of Warsaw from the city. They were "...sent to a transit camp, *Durchgangslager* 121, in Pruszkow. Out of the 350,000 to 550,000 civilians who passed through the camp, 90,000 were sent to labour camps in the Third Reich, 60,000 were shipped to death and concentration camps (including Ravensbrüeck, Auschwitz, and Mauthausen, among others), while the rest were transported to various locations and released." (Zaborksi 2004)

British, American and Polish forces liberated many resistance fighters in POW camps in Germany, and they remained in the West.

The Soviets did not attempt to liberate Warsaw from the Germans until 17 January 1945, when the Red Army, assisted by the First Polish Army, took over the destroyed city. Warsaw suffered damage from the German invasion of Poland in 1939 and the Warsaw Ghetto Uprising of 1943, but nothing could compare with the destruction that occurred in the street fighting of the Warsaw Uprising, which saw 25 per cent of Warsaw's buildings destroyed. After the uprising, German troops systematically burned and demolished another 35 per cent of the city, block by block using flamethrowers and explosives on Himmler's orders:

> The city must completely disappear from the surface of the earth and serve only as a transport station for the *Wehrmacht*. No stone can remain standing. Every building must be razed to its foundation. (Witsuka and Tomaszewsk 2006)

Before the war, Hitler had planned to turn Warsaw into a German city. Now it was to be merely a military transit station. German engineers were despatched to destroy Warsaw, including historical monuments, pieces of art, monuments of science and culture, the national archives and libraries. Nearly a million inhabitants lost all of their possessions.

The Germans reduced Warsaw to smoking ruins, the skeletons of burnt blocks of apartments surrounded by rubble and destroyed bridges sunk into the river. It was like a ghost town.

The Soviets paid the highest price to defeat the Nazis in Europe, losing more than 26 million troops, so the Allies didn't want to upset them, and this accounted for their low-level support for their ally Poland. This lack of support was despite the fact that Polish pilots helped win the Battle of Britain in 1940, 115,000 Poles fought in Italy under British command, and after D-Day Poles fought on the western front. They also fought for Britain in the Middle East.

Tehran Conference

The Tehran Conference sealed the fate of Poland. It was a meeting between US President Franklin D. Roosevelt, British Prime Minister Winston Churchill and Soviet Premier Joseph Stalin in Tehran, Iran, between 28 November and 1 December 1943. It is reported that:

> Stalin pressed for a revision of Poland's eastern border with the Soviet Union to match the line set by British Foreign Secretary Lord Curzon in 1920. To compensate Poland for the resulting loss of territory, the three leaders agreed to move the German–Polish border to the Oder and Neisse rivers. This decision was not formally ratified, however, until the Potsdam Conference of 1945. (Office of the Historian n.d.)

It seems the president of the Polish government-in-exile, Władysław Raczkiewicz, was not aware of this. Also, the Americans were keen to get Soviet support for the war against Japan. At the Yalta conference between the Americans, British and Soviets from 4 to 11 February 1945, the Allies withdrew support for the Polish government-in-exile and Poland was allowed to become a Soviet satellite. Other decisions were made that enabled a Soviet sphere of influence in Europe that led to the Cold War. Stalin said:

> For the Russian people, the question of Poland is not only a question of honor but also a question of security. Throughout history, Poland has been the corridor through which the enemy has passed into Russia. Poland is a question of life and death for Russia. (The Latin Library n.d.)

After the war, Poland became a communist state, and remained so until 1989. One occupying force was replaced by another. The Soviets persecuted the soldiers of the Home Army and the resistance fighters of the Warsaw Uprising as being anti-Soviet. Instead of being honoured as brave fighters, they were maligned. A monument to the Home Army was not built until 1989, when the Soviets lost control of Poland. Instead, the Soviet-backed People's Army was glorified. the People's Commissariat for Internal Affairs (NKVD), Stalin's secret police, or the Office of Security (UB), the Polish political police, captured many Home Army fighters, eradicating opposition to postwar communist Poland. The UB operated from 1945 to 1954. They imprisoned the soldiers on charges such as fascism, and sent many to *Gulags*. However, memories of the uprising and lack of Soviet support for them motivated the Polish labour movement, Solidarity, which led peaceful opposition against the Polish communist government in the 1980s.

In Poland now, 1 August is a celebrated anniversary. On the fiftieth anniversary of the uprising, in 1994, Poland held a ceremony and invited the German and Russian presidents. Russian President Boris Yeltsin didn't attend but German President Roman Herzog visited and was the first German statesman to apologise for German atrocities against Poland during the uprising. US Vice President Al Gore also attended. On 31 July 2004, the Warsaw Uprising Museum opened in Warsaw to commemorate the sixtieth anniversary.

35. Warsaw Uprising

36. Soldiers of the Polish Home Army ride a captured German Panther tank on Aug. 2 1944, during the Warsaw Uprising, photo J Deczkowski

37. Street in Warsaw destroyed during the failed
1944 uprising against Nazi occupiers

12

Told to Go but Where to Hide?

*You know, it's so unjust that we survived so much,
and here we see the freedom already here, and now
we have to die.*

—Lena Goldstein, 1944

The end of the Warsaw Uprising marked the end of Lena's safe hiding place in the Aryan bathroom. After eighteen months of silence and isolation, Lena and her friends were thrown out on the street.

> The Poles couldn't win the war with the mighty Germans because the Germans came back and they [the Poles] surrendered, and the conditions of the truce were that the whole population of Warsaw had to evacuate Warsaw. Any person found in the area of Warsaw would be shot, no questions asked. So, the Poles had to leave. They didn't know there were any Jews left.
>
> So, our benefactor was afraid, if they found out, of what his fate would be. You can't tell the Germans not to open the bathroom, and he was even more afraid of the Poles themselves, so he told us to go.

After all that time! Lena shook her head as if still in disbelief. No longer safe, where would they go? What would they do? Time to face the outside world again. With no money and only the clothes on their backs, nothing to their names. All bereft, all alone except for each other.

Lena writes in an explanation to her diary, the first entry of which is Thursday 16 November 1944:

> Prior to the Warsaw Uprising in September 1944, Hela, Adek, Jake and myself had been hiding in the bathroom of a Polish gentile. When the uprising failed, the entire population of Warsaw was evacuated. To avoid falling into the hands of the Germans and knowing that the Russians were just on the other side of the Vistula [River], we were desperate to find an alternative hiding place. For a few days, in the chaos of the evacuation, we wandered the streets not knowing what we could do.

As they walked along in trepidation, getting more and more desperate for a hiding place, Lena said to Adek, "You know, it's so unjust that we survived so much, and here we see the freedom already here, and now we have to die."

Lena's words had barely been blurted out when a stranger who looked and spoke like a typical Polish peasant came up to them and said in Hebrew, *"Amcha"* (your people).

"It was like a password. And I said, 'Yes.'"

> He looked terrific and, as I told you, like a typical Polish peasant: not just a Pole, but a peasant. Polish peasants have a special look around them, you know. You could see that it's just a simple worker, farmer, something like that. Anyway, he lived all the time as an Aryan on Polish Aryan

papers, and he was selling cigarettes and matches, and nobody was touching him. People would have trays of whatever they were selling.

He built himself a bunker because he thought it would take a few days, so he'll stay and wait for the Russians. But then he didn't know. It might take, he didn't know how long, but he decided he'd risk it again and go off as an Aryan. So, he told us if we want to, he can leave us this bunker of his if we want it.

They couldn't believe their luck. The diminutive Lena felt her spirit rising. "We wanted it! So, he took us there, and he gave us one big suitcase of matches – which are very important – and one big suitcase of cigarettes."

Their new Polish friend led them to a hole, big enough for one person, which descended at an angle for about six metres into one of the canals below the city. At the bottom, Adek and Jake built a raft from the debris of the city. Near the opening, they found a small outcrop of earth – a sort of natural platform, about 2–3 square metres – that their new friend called his bunker. Lena said, "It was like a dugout sitting on the water. There was only enough room that four people could lie next to each other. If you had to walk, you would step over each other. The bunker was a few floors underground, so deep that it was already subterranean water there. So, it was a tiny piece of *terra firma* which was a little bit bigger than this table," she says, pointing to a small table.

On the way there, we met five other Jews that were in the same situation, and they didn't know what to do with themselves, so we offered that they join us, but there was no room for nine people there. Yet Warsaw was in ruins. Everything was in ruins. I mean, everything was bombed, so there was a lot of material, wood and bricks and things like that, which they could scavenge by going back to the surface, so they built a mezzanine, even right there underground. To get to this bunker, they built a raft, so we had to swim to it. There was water in the tunnel. Five people were living upstairs on the mezzanine they constructed and four downstairs on the lower level, because downstairs we also had to find room to dig up a pit for the toilet.

Some bricks were used for a stove. Five beds of hay were prepared for those on the mezzanine floor, and old car seats were used to make beds for those living downstairs. The upstairs group were Jurek and Anna, who were married, Wanda, Michael and Hela. They were all twenty to thirty years old. It was hard to do much when there was no room to stand up and walk.

The people upstairs were living and sleeping but couldn't stand up or walk. It was too small for five. They could either sit or lie down. They made a "mountain chair". I called it a mountain chair because in Poland we have mountains, but you use a string like a harness to go up and down. When they had to come down to us to get the food or go to the toilet, they had to come for it on the mountain chair, on this rope.

Lena and her three friends couldn't stand up either, only sit or lie down, a difficult situation. But they were safely hidden.

Now for food, we stole it. There was not anyone around to steal it from. We stole two sacks of grain from an abandoned brewery. One was rye and one was wheat. You know, there were no people in Warsaw and, after evacuating, nobody had any thought of coming back yet, so that gave us the chance to scavenge. And we stole a coffee grinder. We used it for grinding this grain and boiling it in water. So, we were not allowed to wash for six months because that was our drinking water. And we had only the clothing that we wore when we went into the bunker. I had to wear the same clothes six months day and night without changing. We were full of lice, but we were so lucky that they were not infectious like the ghetto lice.

We changed night to day and vice versa. We couldn't talk too loudly because maybe someone close by would hear. Two people would go in our night, their day, up through the tunnel a few floors because it was very deep and search the deserted houses looking for food and something to clean the water. Also, to check garages for petrol. They got paper for me, and I used a pencil to write. We used fountain pens those days, but we had no ink. I made do.

Amazingly, Lena and the others didn't get sick. "That's what I couldn't understand. It was winter, a very cold winter, and we didn't have warm clothes. In 20 degrees below zero, but we were not cold as we were warming each other." After all this time, Lena still said it with surprise in her voice: "I didn't hear anybody coughing or sneezing. The only sickness anyone suffered with was haemorrhoids, and you know what? I understand. The toilet was right in the middle of downstairs. There were men and women. We had to go to the toilet in front of everybody, and we didn't even have toilet paper, nothing."

Once a week, on their raft, they took the contents of the toilet as far away as they could to get rid of the smell and for hygiene. It was Lena's job to clean the bucket.

As their only food was grain, no vegetables, fruit or meat, nutrition was a problem. "We were swollen," said Lena. "We jokingly told one another we were suffering from obesity. Anyway, we were trying not to go to the toilet, and then we developed haemorrhoids." Lena is now so slim, it is hard to imagine her being large, but those suffering from malnutrition can often appear swollen.

Hidden from the outside world, they could only guess at what was happening – no TV, radio, newspaper, phone or computer; no natural light or electricity, heating or cooling, just the flicker of light from the odd candle they managed to find when foraging. They couldn't see the sky, the sun, the rain, the trees, the buildings or people. What did people on the outside know that they didn't know in the bunker? What would they say if it was possible to talk to them? Did people's faces show worry or fear or bewilderment? How many people were left given that the Germans had made the Poles evacuate Warsaw? They were all alone.

Anastasia Uricher, an architecture student in Sydney made a model of the bunker at Eva's request. The photos are below and Anastasia writes the following to explain her model:

Artist's note: While this model illustrates the very cramped and difficult conditions the group lived in, it cannot capture the drama of an instant disappearance below a destroyed and abandoned Warsaw: the lack of sanitation and toiletries, the humiliation of public toileting and haemorrhoids, the gnawing pangs of starvation, nor the constant itch of lice. This model is a representation of "The Bunker", Lena's hiding space for over six months until WWII came to an end. It is approximately 1:100 in scale. The underground hideout was roughly 1.8m x 1.8m, located on subterranean waters. It was concealed on all four sides with insulation paper to protect the group in the unlikely event someone might happen across the space. Nine people inhabited the hiding spot; four people slept on the "ground floor" on old car seats taken from the derelict garage above, and five slept on the "mezzanine level" on straw sacks. On the "mezzanine level", a hole

123

roughly in the middle of the floor allowed them to use a dangling rope to step "downstairs".

The figures have been deliberately uniform, white and featureless, symbolising the dehumanising impact of the Holocaust. In reality, their clothing was tattered, soiled and torn, as everyone wore what they arrived in until they were able to leave. Washing was not an option, as the fetid water surrounding them needed to be conserved for drinking. Lena and Adash (Adek), popularly referred to as the "Gondolier", were responsible for the weekly dumping of the bucket of human waste. They travelled on a rickety raft, ensuring to paddle out far enough away from their hiding spot that the stench would not divulge its location.

An old tin can with scavenged petrol was placed between two bricks and used to cook their one meal of the day: rations of grain from a sack they had picked up on "the outside". Early on, they acquired wax and something to purify the water with from an old pharmacy aboveground. The man who gave them the location of the bunker also gifted them cigarettes and matches. They smoked to suppress their appetites and used the matches to light the "stove", and they fashioned a candle from wax and a thread from one of the men's suits. Lena used the candle to write the "Bunker Weekly" to lighten the mood and curb group conflict, in rising fear that certain members of the group would leave and disclose their hideout. Although the situation was hopeless, humour became a means of survival.

38. Nine Hiding in the Bunker, Model by Anastasia Uricher

39. Adek and Lena Dispose of Toilet Waste While Others
Remain in Bunker, Model by Anastasia Uricher

13

Lena's Diary and
Bunker Weekly

For us, freedom is a word which has come alive: it is our goal and dream. It is the sky above us and the sun and the stars and the ground under our feet and the air for our lungs. It is a full stomach and a fearless look. It is the end of a hunted dog's existence: everything that we are missing and everything for which we strive. That is freedom; to us freedom means life.

—Lena Goldstein, 1944

Lena's diary

In the isolation, Lena turned to the comfort of writing. What other comfort is there besides the conversation of some fellow humans hiding with her for fear of their lives? She starts her diary on 16 November 1944. She is now twenty-five years old, with death staring her in the face these last five years. She picks up paper and pencil and writes in Polish wistfully:

> I long for the splatter of autumn rain. I long for the monotonous music of raindrops beating with fine drizzle against a window pane; for the

grey, melancholy, clouded November sky. And I long for the thoughts; thoughts at a twilight hour, the thoughts which, sad as they might be, never begin with the words, "If I survive..." and never carry the burden of doubt that all this thinking is empty and pointless, because... I will not survive anyway. Outside the rain is falling.

In the morning when everyone is still engulfed in sleep, and nothing interrupts the silence of the bunker except the muffled snoring of men, from behind the "door" of our bungalow comes a subdued melody of raindrops squeezing through a leaky dome of the shelter and falling into the water. It is a sign from the world outside. Rain is falling... And sometimes (seldom, much too seldom) the silence is pierced by the report from a distant shot, an echo of an explosion or a rhythmical staccato of a machine gun. Again, it is a sign from the outside world. It is proof that the Bolsheviks are close after all, that battles are being waged, but so sluggishly that nothing brings the end any closer.

And this is all we know about the outside world in our seventh week of seclusion and total isolation.

We dream of freedom. Freedom: this word has acquired a magical power, and now it means much more than it ever did before. Its meaning is quite different now from what it used to be. It has ceased to be the cliché invariably linked to its cliché-companions "equality" and "brotherhood". It ceased to be a much over-used slogan meant to appeal to hearts and minds, a slogan which had to be translated and analysed because it had its own language. For us, freedom is a word which has come alive: it is our goal and dream. It is the sky above us and the sun and the stars and the ground under our feet and the air for our lungs. It is a full stomach and a fearless look. It is the end of a hunted dog's existence: everything that we are missing and everything for which we strive. That is freedom; to us freedom means life.

Fortunate are those who believe... They can bend their heads in humility or raise their eyes towards the sky and implore: "Because of all the suffering we endured, because of torments of hopeless longing and inconsolable sorrow, because of countless humiliations, because of the shed tears, because of the load bearing down too heavily upon human beings that we are, we beg you oh Lord to remove the burden from our shoulders and allow us to become human again."

Fortunate are those who believe that their prayer will reach the Almighty being in his justice; that it will be heard and that G-d will, at last, bring their misery to an end.

It is hard for those who do not believe. We cannot lighten the burden of our hearts through prayer, nor can we entrust our worries to someone who will deliver us from them.

Like a miser, I eagerly lock up all that hurts me within the treasure chest of my heart, in order that I may take out, now and then, a penny, and in a flow of frankness entrust it to someone there to listen, and then once again carefully turn the key to lock the chest, for no one can help me. In a crowd of people, one is always alone...always alone...

Later that night, 11 pm, Lena picks up from where she left off. The pain expressed in her writing is added to by the arguments of her companions, especially when they were trying not to be too noisy:

> Apparently, my cup of bitterness is not yet full. At moments like this, I am ready to blaspheme, for I am glad my parents have not lived to see me in my present situation. I grab a pencil so that by writing I would turn my attention from the heated conversation going on around me, but nothing helps. I am burning with shame.
>
> Every second which prolongs our stay together is for me a dance upon red-hot coals.
>
> I cannot find words to describe the storm in my heart. I want to howl and whimper like a dog, for it seems to me that something in my heart will crack, that there will be an explosion. I wish I could change my already stony heart into a hard rock so that I would not react to the stupidity and coarseness of those to whom I am bound by fate.

The following day, Friday 17 November, Lena is starting to find some comfort in her diary, so she picks up pencil and paper again:

> Today Jurek reconciled the two brothers-in-law and at the moment "a small idyll" reigns. But I do not know for how long. However, after that incident, there remains a feeling of bad taste which one cannot neutralise. "It is a bad bird which fouls its own nest."

On Saturday 18 November, Lena made another entry, seeing the comical side of things but worried about starvation:

All that quarrel yesterday, those reproaches about all the sins and mutual offences, committed or not committed, the reckoning about money, becomes more and more comical, yet at the same time painfully tragic in its nonsense, considering our situation. Our food is coming to an end. We calculated that we have enough groats, barley and wheat to last us for about two weeks. Fat will be gone even before that. And then what?

At present, there is no sign of an offensive. Nothing indicates a forthcoming liberation. However, the possibility and diversity of death increase. We are now playing our last card. We are again preparing for looting. Perhaps this time it will prolong our lives again as it has done several times before.

Faced with a threat of fuel shortage, which would stop us from using the remaining food supplies, Jake departed with Anna (on a raft through the canals), and they brought back some kerosene and petrol. When we were threatened with a shortage of candles, a second expedition to the shelters brought us a booty of a kerosene lamp and wax. A third expedition brought once again an abundant loot of fuel, one more kerosene lamp, and even barley and coffee, as well as a head of cabbage. I wonder if the next expedition will prove itself as providential.

Monday 20 November brings more talk of foraging expeditions, despite their danger:

There was no expedition yesterday. We were planning something much more dangerous, namely going outside and reaching any previously inhabited building. Wanda and Hela Domagalska were the ones to go first. That kind of expedition is very dangerous because it threatens their lives and ours. What if they come upon Germans, who might live there now, and the area is forbidden to the civilian population? Then their Aryan looks would not help them at all. Wanda's brother Jurek objects to her going out, while Michael does not allow Hela to join her. Both of them, but particularly Hela, are too chicken to persist. And so, I hear today that the plan has been abandoned. Food is getting more and more scarce, and the situation is going from bad to worse. Everybody's nerves are stretched to the limit. No wonder that arguments and quarrels flare up over trifles. "Something is rotten in the state of Denmark."

And in the morning, a short roar of engines; then a few rap-raps of the anti-aircraft gunfire, and then silence…

Should that bring us hope of life against the spectre of death, which like Damocles' sword hangs incessantly over our heads?

Buried in the bunker in the canals under Warsaw, the sounds of distant battle intrude on Lena's entry of Thursday 23 November:

For the third day, we wake up to the sound of explosions, hum of engines and boom of artillery. All those sounds are muffled and unclear. The reason for it was explained during our last (4th) expedition. The entry to the bunker collapsed at some time in the last few days, leaving us buried and even more cut off from the outside world. In spite of that, the sounds of battle bring us a flicker of hope, but I must confess that as far as my feelings are concerned, I am afraid to let any hope enter my heart. So many times, already, in a similar situation, with our spirits rising... boom!...from the sky back to the earth, painfully bruised in the fall. Is it surprising that I am afraid to let myself hope, so as not to be left with one more disappointment?

In the meantime, in the bunker, further rationing of food to stretch our supplies and allow us to continue for another month. The men are hungry. But not only the men. Is it enough, whether you are a man or a woman, to live on one bowl of "spit" soup and two wheat patties, mixed with water and fried without fat? (This was our ration for 24 hours.)

Hunger and nervous tension usually go together. Everybody became quarrelsome and extremely edgy. To add to our misery a scourge of all kinds of lice, fleas and other insects descended on the scene in plague proportions. This became the last straw in our striving to persevere and endure. Not wanting to deceive ourselves, there is nothing left to us but, while lying on our so-called beds, to listen intently to sounds of war bringing destruction and death, but to us, oh paradox, bringing...who knows? Maybe life?"

Too weak from lack of food to write, Lena didn't make another diary entry until nine days later, on Saturday 2 December. Her discouragement was mounting:

So, what did the last week bring us? It was stormy, full of incidents, but in effect leaving us with a distaste, putting another layer of discouragement upon our hearts.

Last Saturday Hela and I got up determined to leave the bunker at night in order to reach the attic of the house above us and gather "intelligence" information on the current situation. Because all our courageous girls with Aryan looks failed us and the meagre hoard of food was disappearing at an alarming rate, there was no choice but for we two who had the most Semitic appearances to undertake this dangerous mission. As it turned out, our courage was not enough in this case. Should we be caught outside it would endanger all the others. We decided then that in spite of minimal chances of finding anything more in the shelters we have to organise another expedition to do a "final clean-up". Wanda, Jake, and Adek went by raft and returned with totally unexpected results in loot – about 20 kg of food, some sugar, some marinated pumpkin, candle wax, wicks for kerosene lamps and petrol. All that would prolong our lives till about the 1st of January, naturally without the possibility of increasing our present rations. In simple terms, we could say that we have the chance to prolong our starvation for one more month.

On their return, members of the expedition nonchalantly mentioned that they found a sack full of bedding in the bomb shelter. Both Domagalskas, ridiculously greedy for material goods (considering our situation!) jumped up next morning immediately coming up with a suggestion to explore the bomb shelter for some more loot. They did not consider the danger. Were there still any people in the area they could easily trace them to our hiding place. Because of their stubbornness and lack of intelligence trying to persuade them was useless. Arguments, quarrels...*comme toujours*. Nevertheless, we decided that on Tuesday we will still take off. A fever of preparation, big plans and big hopes, as well as a big disappointment. As we found out, the tunnel connecting us to the other shelters – our only outlet – had collapsed. It is possible that someone blocked it from the outside, but more probably the ceiling had given way and filled up the tunnel. We had already been noticing for weeks the debris sifting through the ceiling, possibly as a result of rain forcing its way through the cracks caused through war activities.

So...completely buried...a frightening feeling, especially knowing that food is short and that there is no certainty that the end will come this month since in two months there have been no changes whatsoever. The men decided to open up the tunnel, but they are weakened by hunger to the extent that only the thought of it filled them with fear. And now a new fight broke out, much more serious than the previous ones – most shameful if it were not for the effects of hunger. Of course, the instigator was Jake, with his uncurbed language and his limitless stupidity. As a matter of fact, the basis of Jake's reproaches was mostly right, because from the very first day we entered the bunker, Jurek, Anna and Wanda did not act properly. It is true that they brought with them "luxuries", namely lard, white bread and even canned goods, but the rest of us provided basic foods like rye, wheat, sugar and black bread, which were the bases of our survival until now. However, they, contrary to the decent way, the way we acted, instead of putting it to the common use, kept their food supplies separately, treating it as their own property. Sometimes out of "politeness", they allowed us to partake. That alone caused a certain hostility to creep into our relationship.

When Anna's careless housekeeping caused the food, that should have lasted for a considerable time, to be consumed at a frightening rate, we were forced to consider steps to save the situation. But even then, in spite of the appearance of all food being combined, one could notice that some people were treated more generously than others. This could have passed without comment were we all well fed, but it had to lead to a scene when, alas, everybody is hungry, especially the men. That initiated a "chat" between Jake and Anna, and he was too stupid to progress intelligently. Consequently, once the subject was raised, instead of bringing up appropriate matters he reproached her with leaking margarine on the sly, etc.

It was no wonder that not only Anna felt hurt, but also Jurek, who seems to me to be a man of impeccable character. At the same time, a quarrel took place between Wanda, Michael and his wife. Atmosphere heavy and unpleasant to the extreme. In the end, it was decided that all the women would distribute food, but that was understood to mean Hela and Anna only. But it has to be admitted that things improved since.

But next day again – a fight between Michael, his wife and Wanda. That caused a simply unheard-of attack of hysteria from Wanda, during which she threatened that, should she be forced to leave the bunker, she would not hesitate to denounce us when the first German hit her. Later she tried to justify herself to me and maintain that she would never do it. In reality, she was only threatening to do it so that the others would not dare to provoke her. Nevertheless, the utterance itself was most unfortunate.

Both those quarrels upset Jurek immensely. He felt as I did during the fight between Jake and Adek, namely a certain whine, feeling that the nerves stretched to their limits would not stand the strain, and that in a moment they would break and that an explosion would follow for which one cannot be responsible. Anyway, Jurek, more than the others, cannot cope with the nervous tension in which we live. Lately, the lack of cigarettes had been the last straw as he had always been a heavy smoker. All these fights were nails to his coffin. He decided to leave, together with Wanda. Anna was to stay here. Of course, in their leaving the bunker, there was a greater chance of death than life. He was taking with him his Colt, and I suspect that he wouldn't think twice before putting a bullet to his own head. Naturally, the mood in the bunker is morbid. We all thought that they took the decision to leave the bunker as a direct result of the brawls between Jake and Michael.

Adek had a short talk to Jake and then to Michael, and by the evening peace reigned in the "family", and finally, the would-be deserters decided to stay. But the storms that had passed left a residue of ill-will that made us feel as though

we are all sitting on a volcano that might explode
at any time.

Now, finally, the first day of harmony and
the men left to dig an opening in the tunnel and
try their luck at looting."

After this long entry about their starvation and the nervous tension and quarrels it led to, Lena writes of her heartache for her boyfriend Simon, or Szym. Lena couldn't hold him in her arms, tell him she loved him, see his smile, hear his voice. She could only touch him in her dreams, talk to him in daylight reveries, feel his presence fleetingly. Could she have had a short time of happiness as his wife before the Germans cruelly ended his life? She wrote:

Yesterday, the 1st December, was Szymek's
birthday. I thought of you, my one and only. I
thought how much easier it would have been to
bear my present existence were you here with
me. And I thought that today, as always, as at all
times, I cannot believe that you're not alive anymore, Szym. It was a sad day yesterday. It should
have been your 27th birthday. Your life was too
short. Too early brutal death took you away.
Amongst those few surviving Jews, you would
have been one of the worthy ones. But fate is not
based on justice. Neither does it weigh merits
and values on equal scales. The righteous ones
and the good ones are gone; others remain. The
history of Noah's ark has not been repeated. You
come to me in my dreams, Szym. You come back
in my thoughts and daydreams because longing
for you cries constantly in my heart...

The whole month passed and Lena thought wistfully of the year's end and a new year with no hope in sight. The desire to find her sister

Fela strengthened Lena's will to survive. Lena believed and hoped Fela was still alive. It was Sunday 31 December:

> The last day of 1944. Tomorrow a new year will rise. With melancholy, I live through the sad anniversaries. I don't even try to recall the memories of the New Years of the times gone by. Memories are too painful. One has to live here as if life began with entering this bunker, and as if, except for us, nothing and no one exists in time and space. We were turned into animals to such a degree that nothing, even the worst in our past, would compare with the present. At times it seems to me that in my despair and exhaustion, I am on the verge of insanity, but as a counter-weight to this state of mind, my reason brings forth its own arguments.
>
> There is one goal and one love left in my life. It is Fela. For her, for my sister, for my only living and beloved being, whom, I believe, to be still alive, I want to survive. Only for her sake, I have the will to survive, and only the thought of her gives me the strength to bear all the suffering, for which even the brightest future could not compensate. For her only, I want to live, and consequently, I must not give up. Although lack of energy and resourcefulness are my most serious faults, I have to counter them with patience and a will to survive.
>
> And so, the last day of the year 1944 passes, the sixth year of an unyielding-in-its-brutality war.

In danger of being turned in

There were nine people, malnourished, angry and miserable. "We called them upstairs people," said Lena "and we were downstairs people. They were angry, they were dissatisfied. I mean, they were upset and depressed. They couldn't stand up or walk, move around much. Not everybody can take six months living like that. We were all hungry and itchy. Millions of lice on you." She continued:

> So, they decided to leave. They said they'd rather be killed, and I don't want to live like that, and we're leaving. We couldn't let them leave for two reasons. First of all, one of the men upstairs had a revolver, and he had nine bullets, and we had an agreement with him that if we got caught by the Germans, he's going to kill the eight of us and then he'll kill himself. So, it was not the person, it was the revolver that we couldn't let leave.
>
> That was one thing, and the other thing was that one of those women said, "If they try to torture us, I'm going to turn you in." Afterwards, she was explaining she didn't mean it, she just said it to frighten us, but she said it. And for me, that's enough because that did happen to others, you know. There were no more people in Warsaw so they would be able to find anybody easily.
>
> We didn't know how to keep them in, so I started writing a satirical newspaper that you will see here. My diary, I kept for myself. But this newspaper, it was called *Bunker Weekly*. I was reading them every time I wrote it, and they were laughing because it was satirical. And if it was funny and they were laughing, their anger was gone. And I kept it up for the whole six months."

Lena's humour keeps them alive

Here is an excerpt from the *The Bunker Weekly*.

> Tourist! Now we are entering a canyon, leading us down to the sea level. But here, O traveller, it is not enough to be an erudite or archaeologist. You must also be an accomplished mountain climber. But what is a climb like that to you, you who conquered The Gievont Mountains, Mount Blanc and, who knows, maybe even Mount Everest?
>
> You will descend and squeeze yourself through a crevice. But stop here. Go back in time and remember: Have you ever seen films with Boris Karloff, where there was a warning "People with strong nerves admitted only." If your nerves are too fragile, turn back. Though if you were up to it and decided to continue, you have just entered a land that never knew daylight… Darkness reigns supreme. We shall name the place *Citta della note aeterna* – City of eternal night".

Lena must have had an incredible sense of humour to be able to make them laugh regularly when they were going through such a tough time, not knowing when and how it would end.

At Eva's urging, Lena reads me the story of the turtle:

> I'll read it from the beginning. *The Bunker Weekly*, price: one cigarette. Because did I say that matches were so important, because we had to boil the water, you know. This water had to be boiled because it was there for thousands of years. The cigarettes helped when we were hun-

gry, and we didn't have anything to eat. So, I always thought, it's propaganda against cigarettes because they're killing people, but sometimes they save lives as well. In our case they saved lives.

On this day, I present to you, dear readers, the first edition of our bunker newspaper. Our task will be to inform you about all events of interest to the citizens of our small country. It will contain political and military as well as internal, social, economic and other news. As our paper progresses, we shall also introduce an advertisement section.

It looks very promising, as it has the distinction of being the only newspaper in the world read by all citizens without exception, irrespective of religion, gender, nationality, age and education. The only temporary problem is a chronic shortage of paper, which has a negative influence on the aesthetics of the external appearance. We ask all you people to collect all the pieces of clean paper you come across and hand them over to the editors. The cooperation of the readers will be welcome...

Lena looked at us smiling, "As I told you, we developed, because of the toilet business, haemorrhoids. So, I wrote 'The Suppository and the Turtle'."

There he sat, uncomfortable in his shell; the suppository consorted with the turtle. He replied, "I'd rather stay in my shell than in someone else's arse to dwell."

Lena looked up. "Well, now you're smiling, you're laughing. They were laughing, and that's what kept them there. You know, when they were laughing, they forgot that they had to live their physical lives. But then, back to young housewives."

> And if you have a growing tendency to obesity amongst our readers that can be blamed only on our climate conditions, the Association of Housewives, with the approval of the High Commission, issued an ordinance according to which members of the high society would limit themselves to one, or at maximum two, units a day.
>
> Further, to the ordinance, we are opening to all housewives the following excellent recommendation, what to cook, in the form of a weekly planner. Monday: one bowl of spit soup.

Lena looked up from her *Weekly Bunker* reading to explain. "Why it was called spit soup? We couldn't grind the husks, so the husks needed to soak and we're eating like that, so we call it spit soup. And two patties with coffee. Patties were the same grain, but instead of boiling the water, we were making patties, and we had a big frying pan, and we were frying them without oil, without any fat, you know, and they were the patties. And coffee, we were burning the same grain until it was black, grinding it, and with the water, we were drinking it as coffee. So, one bowl of spit soup, two patties with coffee."

Going back to *The Bunker Weekly*, Lena read:

> Tuesday: two patties with coffee, one bowl of spit soup. Wednesday: One bowl of spit soup, two patties with coffee, and so on and so on. And Sunday: Two patties with coffee, one bowl of spit soup with dumpling.

In case we were wondering she explained, "Dumpling was the same grain but, you know, made as dumpling. But you know what?

Because we didn't have any medicine for haemorrhoids, do you know how we cured it? We were eating this grain; it was mouldy because it was standing it the water."

Eva exclaimed, amazed, "It must have turned into penicillin."

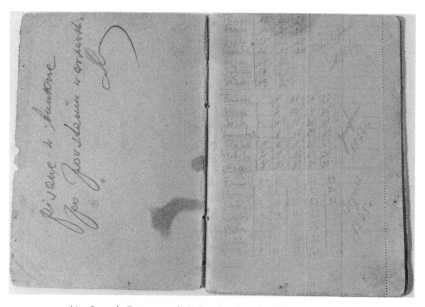

40. Lena's Diary and Calendar Inside View, Currently
Showing in Sydney Jewish Museum

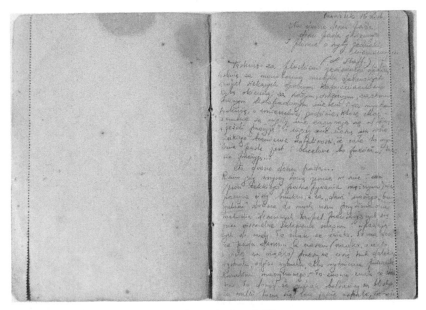

41. Lena's Diary Inside View

42. Lena's Diary Outside View

14

Free at Last

One of our most famous sages – Rashi – said that the only rational explanation for the survival and continuity of the Jewish People – was to believe in miracles.

—Dr Ron Weiser, AM "Nations Bless Israel, April 2018", in *Jews Down Under*

At first, we couldn't believe it. It was impossible to be free… And now, when I knew I could come up [from hiding], I was sitting there crying because in the whole world there was not one person waiting for me and no one to go out to. I was twenty-six years old.

—Lena Goldstein

Freedom came unexpectedly, with little fanfare, even disbelief. Lena sighed.

> And we survived together. Except we didn't even know that we were free. We didn't know that the Russians were here already because we were so deep underground. But one of the women upstairs had a baby that she had to leave behind. She left her baby daughter with a Polish friend of hers

147

because she couldn't take her to the bunker. And so, this Polish friend was the only person in the whole world that knew where we were, or where our bunker was, except for the person who built it. And she came back to Warsaw because people were coming back. Anna wasn't there, so she came to the place that she knew we were hiding and she was singing out, "Anna! Come out! You're free! The Russians are here!"

Finally, Lena was free. All this time she hadn't allowed herself to cry, even with all the death and destruction around her, numb to the never-ending grief. Now tears flooded her. She was unable to hold them back any longer. She was free, but there was no family to greet her. Her sister Fela had disappeared. Was she dead too like the rest of her family? Her boyfriend was dead. It was all so final. There was no one to care that she had survived this horror – no one to go to, no one to welcome her into their homes and hearts. She was all alone. It took Lena a couple of weeks to start to walk upright easily, but it took much longer for the healing of the soul. Lena continued:

> At first, we couldn't believe it. It was impossible to be free. But, you know, she was insistent, so we decided that it's true. We were okay to come out. And at that time, because I lost my parents, I lost my brothers, I lost my whole family, my old friends, everybody I ever knew. I lost them all. All this time, I didn't cry. We didn't cry because we were waiting now for our turn. It's our turn next. And now, when I knew I could come up, I was sitting there crying because in the whole world there was not one person waiting for me and no one to go out to. I was twenty-six years old.

Warsaw was a scene of devastation – gutted four-storey buildings, walls crumbling, windows blown out and piles of rubble. Jews started to return but, even by 1946, all that remained of the Jewish population of Warsaw was 18,000.

Earlier on, they had opened a suitcase in one house, and it was full of money. It was not only Polish money but American dollars, which were a treasure. No one was living there, so they took the suitcase. They buried it in a cellar in the ghetto and hid $200 separately under a staircase in case they needed it to bribe someone.

But when the ghetto was burned, they couldn't get in, and when they did go back, they couldn't find the place. The Ghetto Uprising was on *Pesach* (Passover), and Lena's family had a kosher dinner set used only for *Pesach*. As her parents had been killed in Treblinka, they wouldn't be using it. Just before Lena left the ghetto, a woman asked if she could borrow it, so Lena agreed. Tragically, the woman was killed.

When Adek and Lena and the others went back to look for the buried suitcase, Lena saw the remains of her mother's dinner set scattered among the rubble. It was the remains of her families' life in the ghetto. She tried not to let the memories flood back, the happy times, the sad times, the time her family was destroyed. The kosher dinner set was some evidence they had lived here.

Collecting herself, she thought, "Ah, this must be where the suitcase is hidden." Searching around in the rubble, they were excited to find the suitcase. A cheer went up. But it was empty. Someone else must have been scavenging there. They were crestfallen. It could have helped fund a new life. After all, they had nothing. Lena took one last look at the ruins, the ruins of many lives. They searched under the crumbling staircase and found the $200 Adek had hidden. A smile lit up Adek's face, which had long held a tortured look. They split it up, giving the Polish caretaker of the bathroom money for looking after them. He had returned to Warsaw after the war, as had many other residents.

Lena said, "When we left the bathroom, the Polish caretaker made us swear not to reveal where we had been hiding. It was a condition. It was in the Polish area, and he had beautiful art, probably taken from the ghetto. I'm not sure of his name, maybe Tadek, but his granddaughter was Mary, who became a doctor."

Lena didn't see the Polish peasant again, the one who had allowed them to use the bunker under the canals of Warsaw, but was told he had survived and continued to use Polish papers.

When they came out of the bunker, the houses of Warsaw were in ruins, and most of the windows had broken glass. Adek and Yacov (Jacob) tried to earn money putting new glass in the windows. Lena and other survivors could choose the best abandoned houses in the best position, but all the windows were broken. Lena salvaged glass from a house and put it in the home she chose in one small room that had one window. It was the only room in which someone could live because it was freezing and they needed to keep the wind and cold out. Others stayed there with Lena, huddled together to keep warm. Once they had fixed the window, people from the street saw a room with a window pane and asked if they could sleep for the night. They couldn't say no because people were coming from concentration camps and had nothing.

One of those who sought refuge in that room, Olek, or Alexander, was to become Lena's husband. Like many survivors, he was a pitiful sight. Lena said:

> He was not someone you would immediately find attractive. He had no shirt, a child's jacket, ill-fitting pants and newspapers instead of socks. He was wearing stolen football boots from a dead German soldier. His mouth was swollen because of teeth trouble, but we became good friends. He had been taken to Majdanek, a concentration camp in Poland with his wife and the whole family. They were separated, and he was taken elsewhere. He said he'd have nothing to do with any woman until he found out what happened to his wife. I knew every Jew left alive would contact the Jewish committee. But she was

never found. He had no children as they were newly married.

The Steven Spielberg project to collect and preserve the testimonies of those who survived the Holocaust interviewed him but he didn't want to talk about that part of his experience. Lena explained:

> He lost his first love, though he was a loving husband to me. As a prisoner in the concentration camp, he was making metal components for German arms, so the Germans needed him and brought him extra food. But being a big smoker, he exchanged food for cigarettes. Before the concentration camp, he and his wife were studying commerce at university. He was born on 27 December 1913 but changed his date of birth to 1910 because the Russians would have taken him into the army for five years. This change made him too old.

As she had come out of hiding to freezing weather with only one set of clothes and no coat, Lena's fur coat was essential to her. The Germans said that Jews were not allowed to wear fur. Lena's brother's partner had a nice Polish girlfriend called Zosia. Lena had loaned her fur coat to Zosia instead of giving it to the Germans so, after the war, she could get it back. Lena was in the bunker for six months wearing the same outfit. The temperatures were sub-zero. She was liberated in January, and it was now March. She was freezing.

Lena decided to go to the ghetto to see its present state. On the way, she was excited to see Zosia, who happened to be walking along the street in the fur coat she had loaned her. Lena ran to her.

Puffing and smiling, she said, "I'm so happy to see you. At long last, I'll be warm."

Zosia disdainfully replied, "So what am I going to wear?"

Disappointed again, Lena didn't say a word. She turned around and walked away. It was dangerous to complain. "To kill Jews was like killing a fly," Lena said wryly.

****

The Jewish Committee, established in Warsaw after the war, was a group that was looking for Jewish people and trying to reunite families. A friend of Lena's father contacted her to offer her the opportunity to do volunteer work for them in exchange for food. Lena couldn't go to see him straight away because she had no clothes except the ones she wore when she had left the bunker. So, a representative came to see her and gave Lena clothing for her and her friends. They received clothes from Americans, and among the clothes were flannel pants for women. Lena was shocked. Did women wear pants? Was this a joke?

Lena tried to reconnect families. She was one of the people who had to look for the babies, the children who were taken in and cared for by good people who looked after them while their parents were either killed or in hiding.

Among the people she assisted, Lena saw a girl feeding a baby. She recognised the girl as the best friend of Lena's sister-in-law. After greeting her, Lena asked hopefully, "Have you seen Bronka and Mathis?"

The young woman shook her head, tears rolling down her cheeks. "They were killed in a forest by a Polish smuggler they had paid to help them get away. And their baby too."

Lena put her arm around her to comfort her, "I thought something like that happened but you have a little hope it's not true."

Memories of her brother Mathis came flooding back in this exchange. His kindly look and smiles. She could see his hands that had healed so many as a doctor, his hands that had brought so much life. Now lifeless. The innocent baby that Lena had never been able to scoop up in a hug or sit on her knee. She didn't even know the baby's name or how it had looked. It probably met its fate in Bronka's loving arms, mowed down together. But Lena pushed away the memories to help those who were still alive to help.

Now Lena looked at Eva and me, "You can kill a Jew without any investigation," she said, shaking her head.

****

Despite pushing it down and ignoring it, Lena did feel hurt about anti-Semitism. She said, "This is why Polish Jews were keen to follow socialism or communism because it says everyone is equal. Then we found out it's not like that at all. Jews in Russia had to change their names. The name Goldstein would be dangerous."

There was no traditional wedding for Lena. No family to attend, no beautiful wedding dress, no Rabbi to perform the ceremony, no *chuppah*, or canopy, to be married under, no festive meal and no dancing. It was bereft of much more, including guests to celebrate with the newly married couple. Lena and Alex had lost so much, and this was more disappointment to heap on the coals. It was not safe, even after the war, and they were impoverished because of the Holocaust. But they had each other and a fresh love that would endure.

Lena said, "When I married my husband in Warsaw after the war, it was just a ceremony. We went to the police station and took one friend with us, no documents. Alexander Goldstein was my husband's name, but Okón was the name we used to get married. When in Germany afterwards, we changed it to Goldstein. In Yad Vashem, I'm Helena Okón."

Her second job for the Jewish Committee was to be a correspondent, as she knew several languages (seven if you include Latin). At school, she learned French. In the ghetto, she learned German and Russian. As she couldn't work officially in her early days in the ghetto, she taught herself English from a book. She could understand Yiddish. Lena explained:

> In communist Russia, you were not allowed
> to have any contact with people abroad, because if

you write them letters and you get letters or telephone calls or something, then they consider you a spy. The Jewish Committee was receiving a lot of letters now in different languages, and because I could speak many languages, they gave me an official job to be a foreign correspondent. That is, someone who could write in other languages to correspond with people overseas. It wasn't to do with being a journalist. People wanted to know if anybody survived in their family and, in whatever language, I had to answer. There was mostly one answer: "Sorry, but no one survived in your family." It was heartbreaking to have to give that reply.

Lena's heart was pining for her lost sister, sent to Siberia. But where? It is a big place. But along came a ray of hope, although it didn't seem so hopeful at the time.

One day, a Russian Jewish soldier came to the committee, and he had to go the next day back to Russia. He needed to write a letter to overseas somewhere but Russians were not allowed to communicate with the West. So, he wanted to send it that day from Poland and, because it was from the Jewish Committee, it was an official letter. They sent him to me, and he asked me to write the letter. As I'm writing that letter, he was so grateful to me that he wanted to pay me. I told him, "You can't pay me. That's my job."

But he just sat there. And I didn't know how to get rid of him, and I said... "Oh no, wait. I'll tell you what I'll do. I'll write a letter in Polish, and you take it with you to Russia because, like here, they have an organisation that looks after the asylum seekers. It's called the Organisation of Friends of Polish Patriots." Why patriots, I don't know. That was the name. I said you go to this organisation because I had already written letters galore to every big city that I knew. Do you know all the cities in Russia? I knew most of them. I knew Kiev, I knew Odessa, I knew Stalingrad, Leningrad, but I couldn't know all the cities in Russia, and I never got a confirmation from anybody that they got a letter.

So, I said, "Wherever you go, you just go there to that organisation, show them my letter and wait like you sit here and don't want to move. Don't move until you see that they send me an answer."

Lena remembers the day, "I just wanted to know whether they were alive. Because we had a list of all the survivors, so they should have a list, and know whether my sister and my brother are on it. He promised. And I thought, a young man like that, today he's grateful, and tomorrow he'll forget. He didn't forget. He went to a place that was called Molotov. It never existed before. Molotov was the foreign minister of Russia and they changed the name of another place, in his honour, to Molotov."

The city renamed Molotov after the Russian foreign minister from 1940 to 1957 was Perm, and it was close to the Ural Mountains. Its zoo is home to rare snow leopards and Amur tigers. In the nineteenth century, Perm became an important cultural centre, but its remoteness meant it was used as one of the Russian Empire's many places of exile. Tolstoy wrote of Count Mikhail Speransky in his novel *War and Peace*. The Count fell out with Alexander I and was exiled there. The Nobel-prize-winner Boris Pasternak lived and wrote his novel *Dr Zhivago* in Perm, calling it *Yuryatin*. Because of the name change, it is not surprising that Lena couldn't track her sister down.

"That's where he went," continued Lena, "and he went to this organisation, showed them my letter, and the guy read my letter, and said, 'What! They're my best friends! And they live right here.'"

Miracles

Lena's eyes brightened and she couldn't contain her excitement, "That's one miracle after another. First one, that for the little bit of soup that my father was sharing with the old man I'm still alive. And then, because of that stupid letter, I found my sister."

Lena shakes her head, still amazed. She sees it as a miracle that she was not killed in Treblinka death camp like her parents, a miracle that she didn't die in the Warsaw Ghetto Uprising like her brother, escaping just before it, a miracle that the German guards let her through when so many had been shot trying to escape.

It was a miracle that, because she and her father shared their starvation rations with the old man, she had a bathroom to hide in with his family, a miracle that the Germans did not capture them hiding there for eighteen months.

More miracles are that they met a Jew passing as a Polish peasant, who offered them his bunker when they had to leave the first hiding place, and a miracle Lena and fellow survivors were able to survive on the meagre rations stolen from empty houses as they holed up in a bunker in the canals below Warsaw.

And, through the miracle of a chance meeting with a Russian Jewish soldier who just happened to be stationed in an obscure town in Siberia, Lena found her sister Fela.

Eva agrees, "Many miracles kept you alive."

Lena sees it as a miracle that her sister found her husband at a train station near Brest and that she didn't marry her boyfriend in the ghetto, as the Germans killed him in the gas chambers and she may have been killed with him.

Poland today

Catholic clergy were not immune from imprisonment or persecution, and the Germans sent many to their deaths in concentration
camps.

Author Mark Smith visited Poland in recent years and interviewed
Michael Schudrich, Chief Rabbi of Poland. He talked animatedly
about Jews coming out from hiding their identity or discovering it and
contacting him. He said, "But you have to remember 50 years ago,
95% of Poles were anti-Semitic. Now that figure is probably down to
15%." (Smith 2010)

He gave two reasons: one that Poland was the centre of the Jewish
world with a vibrant community, and they were one-third of the
population, living in a multicultural society. Then the Germans massacred 90 per cent, leaving about 350,000 Jews. He continued:

> Then, after the war, communism came and
> it was made clear that if you were Jewish you had
> to leave the country. In the 25 years after the war,
> about 250,000 Jews left. That means 100,000
> stayed but they went underground and they kept
> their religion, their culture and their heritage
> secret. (Smith 2010)

Since the fall of communism in 1989, children and grandchildren
of survivors are finding their roots. Asked what the second factor was,
Schudrich replied:

> Pope John Paul did an extraordinary thing –
> he declared that anti-Semitism is a sin. They even
> have a national Judaism day in Poland now. I can't
> begin to tell you the impact that had. Almost over-
> night, centuries of anti-Semitism were reversed.
> (Smith 2010)

43. Lena Midler

44. Olek (Alex) Goldstein Before and After Concentration Camp

15

Australia, Place of Refuge

After coming from war-ravaged Warsaw in 1949, where life was still dangerous for Jews, I was amazed when friends told me to visit the Domain [a public park in Sydney] where speakers were standing on soapboxes talking about anything and everything. It was truly an amazing experience to discover this freedom.

—Lena Goldstein

For us, freedom is a word which has come alive: it is our goal and dream.

—Lena Goldstein's diary

Coming from the fear-stricken world she had lived in as a young Jewish woman under Nazi occupation, Lena was awestruck by the freedom she found in Australia. A friend took her to Sydney's Domain but didn't say why. Every Sunday in the Domain, people would get up on their soapboxes and give speeches on anything that stirred them up, trying to influence public opinion. Lena was amazed. Looking on, instead of throwing them in jail or worse, police were protecting them from hecklers instead of accosting them.

> My husband and I saw all those boxes, and
> on every box was somebody speaking against

something. I couldn't understand it coming from Poland. After leaving Poland, we were in Germany for two years in a displaced persons camp. I was afraid there too. I couldn't say anything to a Russian because they would send you to a Gulag or kill you. Friends begged us not to post any news back to Warsaw because of fear. Yet I saw policemen walking past in Australia, smiling. I can't understand them laughing.

I said to Olek, "This is freedom! When I saw that, I fell in love with this country." And it is a love that has continued ever since.

Even getting to Australia had been a journey. After staying in Poland for some time, working with the Jewish Committee and deciding on what may lay ahead, they went to Germany, for a time in the displaced persons camp. From there, they made their way across Germany to Stuttgart, where they found Lena's sister who had given birth to a daughter, Giza.

It was an emotional reunion. The sisters hugged and cried. They had thought they would never see each other again. The embers of the Holocaust would continue to affect their lives well into the future. But Lena had some family after all, and she could hug this beautiful baby without fear of losing her.

From there they made their way to Toulouse, France, where Olek had a brother. The brother had been told to leave Poland before the war due to his political views but had been returned by the Germans to Auschwitz concentration camp. Surviving the harsh conditions there, he went to France. From there, they hoped to escape Europe.

Lena was helped to come to Australia in 1949 by a cousin who had been lucky enough to have been sent here before the war. Lena came with Olek (Alex), miraculously a survivor of three concentration camps, her sister Fela, brother-in-law Ignas and their daughter Giza, who was by then two years old. Alex set up a metal factory in Australia. He and Lena had many happy years together until he died in 2007. They had two children, Stanley and Martin, and five grandchildren.

Telling the story of survival

Lena is not only a survivor; she is also someone who's been very active in telling her story so people would know the truth about the things she has been through and not forget. She shares her story so that it won't happen again. Lena said she would have written more in her diary, but she was either too hungry or too weak to do it.

However, for a long time Lena couldn't share her story. It was too hard, and she was trying to lead a normal life – to rebuild a new life in a new country and raise a family. Journalist Fiona Harari wrote:

> Like many others, she remained silent in the postwar years as she and her late husband Alex, also a survivor, concentrated on living. Long after arriving in Australia in 1949, and a delay of more than a decade in having children for fear of losing them too, Goldstein began having nightmares. Where could she hide her boys in Sydney if they were hunted? It was not until the 1990s that she finally spoke up, recording her story for posterity with Steven Spielberg's Shoah Foundation. Having spoken once, she found she could talk again. (Harari 2015)

Some survivors don't want to remember but can't forget. The past is always there. They live with it, sleep with it and face the day with it, feeling there's no escape from the memories. Some shared little, not wanting to traumatise their families by talking about the Holocaust. They even played it down, but listeners still thought they were exaggerating. However, for some survivors, the desire to tell their stories is just as pressing as the desire to forget. This book is about Lena's promise to her brother to tell people what happened so that the world would know. It is also about the cry of those who didn't make it to "remember me".

In looking at profiles of survivors, Dr Yael Danieli, Director of the Group Project for Holocaust Survivors and Their Children, identified, in 1981, "four types of families of survivors: victim families, numb families, fighter families and families of 'those who made it'" (Portney 2003). Dr Portney said Holocaust survivors who became parents sometimes experienced traumatic reliving of events or emotional numbing or detachment from experiences, putting life in different compartments. These reactions "do not help a child develop a reasonable sense of safety and predictability in the world". (Portney 2003)

A person who experiences or sees a terrifying or traumatic event can experience post-traumatic stress disorder (PTSD) affecting their mental health and well-being. Symptoms can include nightmares, flashbacks and severe anxiety. One woman, a child of a survivor, commented on how post-traumatic stress disorder (PTSD) experienced by some Holocaust survivors was passed on to children and grandchildren, becoming intergenerational trauma:

> Keeping their children — whether born during, at, or after the end of World War II — safe and protected from the world was a common theme for families of Holocaust survivors. Most second-generation survivors, or "2Gs" as we call ourselves, grew up in highly overprotective environments and were allowed few freedoms. Constant location checks were the norm and some of us rarely went anywhere without our parents — or at least without strict supervision.
>
> As my 2G cohort entered adulthood and became parents, we continued the cycle of intergenerational trauma with our children. (Cohen 2018)

There is an incredible resilience of Holocaust survivors considering the dehumanising treatment they have come through. Hypervigilance or screening the environment for threats, fear something would happen to their children, sleep disturbance, irritability and flashbacks are common to those suffering PTSD. Some survivors describe hardening themselves to protect themselves from emotional pain so they could cope with life. They had to learn to trust people again.

Continuity is a big issue. Life was cruelly interrupted. They lost their childhoods, their innocence and their families. The Holocaust robbed them of education and careers. Some survivors have no photos of family pre-Holocaust and memories of what they looked like fade. Lena was able to escape with a few precious photos. Children of survivors can grow up with no uncles or aunties or grandparents to love them. Having grandchildren is very important to most survivors. Jews killed in the Holocaust were deprived of all the descendants they could have had, amounting to generational genocide.

Like many other survivors, Lena has learned not to pity herself or think too much about what she has lost, as it doesn't help. She has learned to look on the bright side of life, and having an adoring family these days helps a lot.

Lena awarded a medal

Lena was awarded an OAM (Medal of the Order of Australia) in 2014 for service to the community and to the Sydney Jewish Museum. She started volunteering at the museum in 1992, the same year it was established, and was involved from the commencement of the "Remember Me" program, which is a monthly presentation by Shoah survivors. Since 2005, she has been a member of the Support Group for Survivor Guides. Telling their stories takes its toll, causing them to be drained or giving them sleepless nights, but the support group has been cathartic. Sometimes they laugh, sometimes they argue, but they have become a family. Lena tells her story for the sake of all the people she loved but who didn't make it. Even at one hundred years old, Lena goes to meetings where she shares her story. Eva Engel usually drives her there.

Lena has been a volunteer presenter at Courage to Care, part of *B'nai Brith*, since 1999. It takes its anti-bullying program to schools and other organisations all over New South Wales and now interstate. Through survivor stories, a short film, an exhibition of artefacts and photos, role plays and group discussions, children are encouraged not to be bullies, bullied or bystanders. Stories of the Righteous among the Nations are exhibited at the Museum and Courage to Care and, although William Cooper is not eligible to be a Righteous Among the Nations, he is included in the exhibitions. He was an Aboriginal Christian, who led the Australian Aborigines League in a protest against *Kristallnacht* to the German consulate in Melbourne in 1938. This was remarkable considering Aborigines were not citizens in their own nation till the 1960s. (Miller 2012)

Despite having shared her story many times, Lena said: "Every time I speak, there's a moment where I can't talk anymore. I don't know why. I always thought that if you talk so many times about something it becomes normal. But it doesn't."

Survivors like Lena often didn't tell their stories earlier because of the pain, not wanting to burden their children, not being ready to or the lack of interest of society. Now with Holocaust studies as part of the school curriculum and the need for survivor guides at the Sydney Jewish Museum, the need for it is there. Lena is one of about thirty survivors who tell their stories as guides at the Sydney Jewish Museum.

Lena lived in Dover Heights, Sydney, when I interviewed her in January 2016, and it was not until September 2017, at the age of 98, that her family insisted Lena go to a nursing home after a car accident. She was not seriously hurt. Until then she was living independently and quite active. Her unit in the Montefiore home in Sydney is very comfortable and, when Norman and I visited her there a few times in June and July of 2018, she was continually receiving phone calls and visitors, a much-loved matriarch of her family.

Lena insisted on being hospitable and made us a cup of tea when we visited, as she insists on doing for anyone who visits. When Norman offered to move the teacups from the sink where she made the tea to the table we were sitting around, Lena stopped him. "No, I prefer to do things myself. I have seen too many people allow others to wait on them and then they can't do anything for themselves. Use it or lose it," she said firmly. "Never stop working while you can. It's all about attitude," she said, teaching us her life lesson. "I am here with the children of my friends, and I have to look after them, make sure they don't forget their medications, and so on."

We spent a pleasant Sunday afternoon with Lena in her unit in July 2018, family members gathered around her. Lena is hard of hearing but very much in charge. Her son Stanley is a medical doctor, and he is surprised I knew his old work colleague, the late Dr Fred Hollows, the famous eye surgeon.

Two of Lena's grandsons were there and hope to visit us in Cairns. We had already spent an afternoon with one of them, Ron, who photographed Lena's photos for me. Eva arranged this. Eva is someone who gets things done he told us. When Norman and I visited Eva to interview her for an upcoming book, she had organised Paul Green to drop off some photos and a video he had taken of Lena for Courage to Care.

Eva was with us this Sunday afternoon and so too was a young Jewish architecture student, Anastasia and her mother. The student had brought with her a model of what the bunker looked like that Lena and her friends had hidden in. She had attempted a number of times to make a replica with plasticine and other materials but couldn't get it to Lena's satisfaction. Lena was concerned about the nine figures being all white with no clothes. "No," said Lena, "they look like dead bodies, and we had clothes on." Lena also said they were dirty, not being able to wash themselves or their clothes. The model replicated a string for those upstairs to come down to use the toilet, which was on the downstairs of the bunker. So, it was back to the drawing board again for Anastasia with some more changes till

Lena finally approved the bunker model in December with the white plasticine figures. As Eva had requested it, she now holds the model.

I asked Lena what helped her survive mentally. I didn't expect the answer I received:

> I never sat down and thought about it. It was natural. I loved all my family but never cried. Next was my turn. Waiting. I didn't believe in life after death. I'm losing all the people I love and knew I'd lost everyone. I don't remember others crying either."

This may itself be a survival strategy and a protective mechanism. Lena seemed to treasure a book called *The Righteous, How the Poles Rescued Jews*, by G. Gorny and J. Rosik. "It is about Poles who risked their lives to save people like me," she explained, and her thoughts went to Magda Szubanski's book *Reckoning: A Memoir*, where she wrote about her father being a Polish assassin, killing Poles who collaborated with the Nazis. I told her I had read Magda's book and found it very interesting. Knowing that many Poles risked death to save Jews like herself helped Lena to deal with the Poles who killed Jews like her brother and his family.

Fiona Hariri, who wrote about many Australian Holocaust survivors, including Lena, visited Warsaw and amazingly found Lena's house still standing today among the ruins. She writes:

> An above ground unit with a view to an internal courtyard, it outlasted the city's tumultuous past, as it continues to do, although it is no longer the comfortable place of her memories. An abandoned space within an old apartment block, it is locked up and weed-strewn and cut off from its former neighbourhood by a newish major road. (Harari 2015)

She also checked out the bathroom where Lena and her friends had hidden for eighteen months, depending on the Polish landlord to bring them food daily. "Across town, the stranger's bathroom in which she cowered has also survived, an anonymous apartment with its silent history as an unlikely haven." (Harari 2015)

Lena's hiding place in a bunker under the city of Warsaw, where she had hidden for about six months is, of course, in disuse but, above it, all has changed. Harari writes:

> And the square beneath which she existed for half a year in a foetid space of air and dirt has been cleared of rubble, and, like so much of the capital's UNESCO-recognized historic centre, has been carefully restored with a shiny Starbuck's outlet competing for attention with alternating neon signs for expensive watches. The modernist American and gracious Swiss embassies lie just metres away from this place that was once cut off from the world. Now the world gathers here to eat and shop and take in a city's unique history. (Harari 2015)

The irony of the Holocaust is that it touched the conscience of the world to support the formation of the modern state of Israel. There has been Arab opposition, and Israel has had to fight many wars to keep its state from being wiped out. In 2018, we celebrated seventy years since the re-formation of the state of Israel, which was formed more than 3000 years ago.

Aviva Wolff of the Sydney Jewish Museum enthusiastically told me that my book on Lena needed to be ready to launch around Lena's one hundredth birthday on 31 January 2019. I had just given a well-attended lecture there in July 2018 on my memoir.

This is not just another story of a Holocaust, or Shoah, survivor. Lena is a remarkable woman. She could have been a lawyer or a writer herself. However, she has made her mark on the world by sharing her story, teaching others about the courage to care, not to stand by and let persecution happen but to stand up for the bullied, the intimidated, the persecuted, and not allow the suffering to occur. Lena showed a remarkable will to survive despite all the hardships. She saved others much mental anguish by her sense of humour in appalling conditions, not knowing if she would survive herself. She is an inspiration to those who have faced unbearable suffering.

She is a loving mother and grandmother to a wonderful family, who are talented in their own right. She loved her husband, who himself had a difficult road to recovery from his appalling treatment by the Nazi machine. She has mentored other Shoah survivors in telling their stories and been a stalwart of the Sydney Jewish Museum, Courage to Care and the Sydney Jewish community generally.

How many children has she helped protect from a life of being bullied at school, by telling her story and urging children not to be bullies, not to be bullied and not to stand by and do nothing? Now through this book, her story can reach around the world and to future generations and continue to inspire people to be their best and treat others well.

45. Lena's Sister Fela and Husband Ignas

46. Lena and Alex Goldstein, 1959

47. Lena Goldstein

48. Lena and Alex Goldstein, 1969

49. L-R Back Row –Martin Goldstein, Lena's son, Werner Charny,
(the Charnys are Vivian's parents)
L-R Middle Row – Vivian Goldstein, Martin and
Vivian's sons Daniel and Jonathan
L-R Front Row – Sylvia Charny, and Lena Goldstein
at Lena's grandson Daniel's bar mitzvah 2005

50. Lena Goldstein with then New South Wales
Governor Marie Bashir at Government House when
Lena received the Order of Australia Medal 2014

51. . L-R Back Row-Lena's grandsons, Ron and Ben Goldstein,
son Stanley Goldstein and grandson Guy Goldstein
Front Row-Eva Engel, Dina, mother of the grandsons, Lena and
author Barbara Miller at Montefiore Home, Sydney 2018

52. L-R Front Row Norman and Barbara Miller, Eva Engel,
Dina, mother of the grandsons and Lena,
L-R back row Lena's grandson Ron Goldstein, son Stanley
Goldstein and grandson Guy Goldstein 2018

Glossary

Agudat Yisra'el Union of Israel, a political movement of Orthodox Jewry.

Anschluss The integration that resulted from German annexure of Austria.

Arbeitslager Forced-labour camp.

Armia Krajowa (AK) Polish underground army. (early chapters)

Armia Krajowa Polish Home Army, or citizen army. (later chapters)

Armia Warszawa Polish Warsaw Army.

Bar Mitzvah It refers a Jewish religious and family commemoration on a boy's 13th birthday after which he is obliged to fulfil all the commandments prescribed to Jews and accept his religious responsibilities as an adult.

Bund Jewish socialists.

Chuppah Wedding canopy.

Erev Pesach Passover eve.

Grossaktion Literally, Great Action, deportation campaigns against the Jews.

Grosze Pennies

Gulag The government agency in charge of the Soviet forced labour camp system for perceived enemies of the government and criminals set up under Vladimir Lenin and built up during Joseph Stalin's rule from the 1930s to the 1950s; similar to a prison in the respect that criminals were often forced to serve their time in "corrective" camps rather than penitentiaries or jail.

Haggadah The text recited at the Seder on the first two nights of the Passover, including the story of the Exodus.

Herrenvolk The idea of a pure German race, misnamed 'Aryan'.

Himmelfahrtstrasse Literally, Street to Heaven, the path to the gas chambers.

Jude Jew in German.

Judenrat Jewish Council.

Judenrein Cleansed of Jews.

Juden Reglements Edict when Warsaw became part of Prussia in 1796 that only allowed Jews living in Warsaw before 1796 to stay in the city

Kabbalah An esoteric school of thought in Judaism.

Kaddish Prayer for the dead, or mourner's prayer; a prayer for the sanctification of God's name and can be said at funerals and by mourners. Sons are required to say *Kaddish* for eleven months after the death of a parent.

Kapo Prisoners in the Nazi concentration camps that helped their captors control the general prisoner population in exchange for privileges.

Kosher Food or premises that satisfy the requirements of Jewish law.

Kristallnacht Literally, the Night of the Broken Glass, 9–10 November 1938

Lagerältester Senior prisoner supervisor

Lalke Doll in Yiddish

Leśni Polish partisans.

Matzot Unleavened bread.

Menorah A seven-branched lampstand made of gold used in the temple in biblical times; a symbol of Israel since ancient times; the emblem on the coat of arms of the modern state of Israel.

Pesach Passover.

Pluj-zupa Literally, spit-soup, made from grinding barley boiled with water, with the consumer needing to spit out the hulls of the grain.

Pogroms Anti-Semitic violence, often large scale and sanctioned by authorities, against Jews, with physical destruction of Jewish property, looting of Jewish homes and businesses and usually involving massacres.

Powstanie Warszawskie The Warsaw Uprising.

Seder Order of service.

Sonderkommando Prisoners, usually Jews, who were forced, on threat of their own deaths, to aid with the disposal of gas chamber victims during the Holocaust.

Talmud The main text of Rabbinic Judaism and the primary source of Jewish religious law and teaching.

Tarnung Camouflage.

Tisha B'Av 9 Av on the Jewish calendar, a day marked by fasting and sorrow because of past persecution and tragedy.

Umschlagplatz Rail station at Warsaw Ghetto used to transport Jews to Treblinka.

Untermensch Subhuman.

Wehrmacht German armed forces.

Yeshiva A Jewish college or seminary focusing on traditional religious texts.

Yiddish A language Jews in central and eastern Europe used before the Holocaust, which has some German, Hebrew and Aramaic influence. It still has some 200,000 speakers, mainly in the US, Israel and Russia and a few in Australia

Yom Kippur The Day of Atonement, the holiest day in the Jewish calendar, is a day of fasting and repentance. It is a serious time of personal reflection as Jews ask G-d to allow them to live another year (be written into the Book of Life).

Zegota The Council to Aid the Jews, set up in 1942.

Zydowska Organizacja Bojowa (ZOB) The Jewish Fighting Organisation, a resistance movement in the Warsaw Ghetto.

Zydowski Zwiazek Wojskowy (ZZW) The Jewish Military Union, a resistance movement in the Warsaw Ghetto.

References

Avigan, Ailsa (2018), *A Neighborhood Favor Platform,* http://www.alisaavigan.com/neighborhood-service-platform

BBC World News (2016), "Last Treblinka Death Camp Survivor Samuel Willenberg Dies", 20 February, https://www.bbc.com/news/world-europe-35623492

Black, Peter R. (2006), "Police Auxiliaries for Operation Reinhard", in David Bankier, ed., *Secret Intelligence and the Holocaust*, Enigma Books

Blakeney, Michael (1985), *Australia and the Jewish Refugees* 1933–1948, Sydney: Croom Helm Australia, p. 131

Borzykowski, Tuvia (1976), *Between Tumbling Walls*, 2nd edition, Hakibbutz Hameuchad Publishing House, p. 57, quoted in Yad Vashem, "The Last Passover in the Warsaw Ghetto", Voices from the Inferno, http://www.yadvashem.org/yv/en/exhibitions/warsaw_ghetto_testimonies/last_passover.asp

Chabad.org (2018), "What Happened on the Ninth of Av?", https://www.chabad.org/library/article_cdo/aid/946703/jewish/What-Happened-on-the-Ninth-of-Av.htm

Chrostowski, Witold (2004), *Extermination Camp Treblinka*, London: Vallentine Mitchell, p. 37

Cohen, Emily, (2018), "Intergenerational Trauma and the Holocaust", Scribe, https://forward.com/scribe/395287/intergenerational-trauma-and-the-holocaust/

Fallet, Mareike, and Kaiser, Simone (2009), "Concentration Camp Bordellos: 'The Main Thing Was to Survive at All', Spiegel Online, http://www.spiegel.de/international/germany/concentration-camp-bordellos-the-main-thing-was-to-survive-at-all-a-632558.html

Gangi, Robert (2015), "Death Camp Treblinka Survivor Stories Documentary", https://www.youtube.com/watch?v=KqLME0OP9cQ

Gasior, Mariusz (2018), "Daily Life in the Warsaw Ghetto", Imperial War Museum, https://www.iwm.org.uk/history/daily-life-in-the-warsaw-ghetto

Gibianskii, Leonid, and Naimark, Norman (2004), *The Soviet Union and the Establishment of Communist Regimes in Eastern Europe, 1944–1954: A Documentary Collection*, The National Council for Eurasian and East European Research, pp. iii, 12, 52, quoted in Wikipedia, https://en.wikipedia.org/wiki/Warsaw_Uprising

Gilbert, Martin (1986), *The Holocaust: The Jewish Tragedy*, London: St Edmundsbury Press

Gutman, Israel (2012), *Resistance: The Warsaw Ghetto Uprising*, Houghton Mifflin Harcourt; Kindle Reprint edition

Hall, Allan (2010), "Confiscated Jewish wealth 'helped fund the German war effort'", *The Telegraph*, 9 November, https://www.telegraph.co.uk/news/worldnews/europe/germany/8119805/Confiscated-Jewish-wealth-helped-fund-the-German-war-effort.html

Harari, Fiona (2015), "'I See My Mum': The Sydney Room Where Holocaust Survivors Share Their Stories", *Good Weekend*, *WA Today*, 27 January

Harari, Fiona (2018) *We Are Here: Talking with Australia's oldest Holocaust survivors,* Scribe Publications

History.com Editors (2009), "Deportations from Warsaw Ghetto to Treblinka Begin", https://www.history.com/this-day-in-history/deportations-from-warsaw-ghetto-to-treblinka-begin

Intrepid Berkley Explorer (2018), "Warsaw's Jewish Heritage: Poland", http://intrepidberkeleyexplorer.com/Page28J.html

Jewish Virtual Library (2018a), "Adam Czerniakow 1880–1942", https://www.jewishvirtuallibrary.org/adam-czerniakow

Jewish Virtual Library (2018b), "Jewish Resistance: Mordecai Anielewicz's Last Letter (April 23, 1943)", https://www.jewish-virtuallibrary.org/the-last-letter-from-morde

Jewish Virtual Library (2018c), "Treblinka Concentration Camp: History and Overview", https://www.jewishvirtuallibrary.org/history-and-overview-of-treblinka

Jewish Virtual Library (2018d), *Virtual Jewish World: Warsaw, Poland"*, https://www.jewishvirtuallibrary.org/warsaw-poland

Lanchin, Mike (2014), "SS *St Louis*: The Ship of Jewish Refugees Nobody Wanted", BBC World Service, St Louis, https://www.bbc.com/news/magazine-27373131

Mackay, T (2016), "Inside the Siege of Warsaw", Recollections of Artur Ney, The Holocaust Survivor Memoirs Program, Azrieli Foundation, http://memoirs.azrielifoundation.org/articles-and-excerpts/inside-the-siege-of-warsaw

Miller, Barbara (2012), William Cooper, *Gentle Warrior: Standing Up for Australian Aborigines and Persecuted Jews*, Xlibris, p. 184

Music and the Holocaust (n.d.), "Treblinka", World ORT, http://holocaustmusic.ort.org/places/camps/death-camps/treblinka/

Narunsky, Gareth (2018), "MPs Apologise for Evian", *The Australian Jewish News*, 5 April, https://www.jewishnews.net.au/mps-apologise-for-evian/75361

Office of the Historian (n.d.), "The Teheran Conference, 1943", US Department of State, https://history.state.gov/milestones/1937-1945/tehran-conf

Portney, Charles, MD (2003), "Intergenerational Transmission of Trauma: An Introduction for the Clinician", *Psychiatric Times* 20(4), http://www.psychiatrictimes.com/comorbidity-psychiatry/intergenerational-transmission-trauma-introduction-clinician

Quora (2017), "How Much Gold Did the Nazis Steal from the Jews?", https://www.quora.com/How-much-gold-did-the-Nazis-steal-from-the-Jews

Romanov, Sergey (2006), "Richard Glazar on Jean-Francois Steiner", in Holocaust Controversies: What Part of the Word Genocide Do You Not Understand?, http://holocaustcontroversies.blogspot.com/2006/10/richard-glazar-on-jean-francois.html

Scrapbookpages.com (1998), "Treblinka Death Camp", last updated 2009, https://www.scrapbookpages.com/Poland/Treblinka/introduction.html

Smith, Mark S. (2010), *Treblinka Survivor: The Life and Death of Hershl Sperling*, Gloucestershire: The History Press

Steiner, Jean-Francois (1994), "Treblinka", in *Treblinka Death Camp*, Plume Publishers, quoted in https://www.scrapbookpages.com/Poland/Treblinka/introduction.html

The Latin Library (n.d.), The Yalta Conference (1945), http://www.thelatinlibrary.com/imperialism/notes/yalta.html

The Treblinka Perpetrators, An Overview of the German and Austrian SS and Police Staff (2006) http://deathcamps.org/treblinka/perpetrators.html

United States Holocaust Memorial Museum (2018a), "Invasion of Poland, Fall 1939", Holocaust Encyclopaedia, https://www.ushmm.org/wlc/en/article.php?ModuleId=10005070

United States Holocaust Memorial Museum (2018b), Resources for Students, https://www.ushmm.org/learn/students/learning-materials-and-resources/poles-victims-of-the-nazi-era/polish-resistance-and-conclusions

Wituska, Krystyna, and Tomaszewsk, Irene (2006), *Inside a Gestapo Prison: The Letters of Krystyna Wituska, 1942–1944*, Wayne State University Press, p. xxii, quoted in Wikipedia, https://en.wikipedia.org/wiki/Warsaw_Uprising

World Jewish Congress (2018), "Museum of the History of the Polish Jews to Open", http://www.worldjewishcongress.org/en/news/museum-of-the-history-of-polish-jews-to-open

Yad Vashem (2018a), "Clearing the Ruins of the Ghetto", Voices from the Inferno, http://www.yadvashem.org/yv/en/exhibitions/warsaw_ghetto_testimonies/gesia_camp.asp

Yad Vashem (2018b), "Fighters in the Warsaw Ghetto", Mordechai Anielewicz, 23 [21] April 1943, Voices from the Inferno, http://www.yadvashem.org/yv/en/exhibitions/warsaw_ghetto_testimonies/fighters.asp

Yad Vashem (2018c), *"Hell has Come to Earth" An Anonymous Woman's Diary from the Warsaw Ghetto Uprising*, p. 30, in "The Liquidation of the Warsaw Ghetto", Voices from the Inferno, http://www.yadvashem.org/yv/en/exhibitions/warsaw_ghetto_testimonies/liquidation.asp

Yad Vashem (2018d), "January 1943: The First Armed Resistance in the Ghetto", Voices from the Inferno, http://www.yadvashem.org/yv/en/exhibitions/warsaw_ghetto_testimonies/resistance.asp

Yad Vashem (2018e), "The Last Passover in the Warsaw Ghetto", Testimony of Shoshana Baharir, Yad Vashem Archive, O.3/5469, http://www.yadvashem.org/yv/en/exhibitions/warsaw_ghetto_testimonies/last_passover.asp

Zaborski, Zdzisław (2004), *Tędy przeszła Warszawa: Epilog powstania warszawskiego: Pruszków Durchgangslager 121, 6 VIII – 10 X 1944* (in Polish), Warsaw: Askon, p. 55, quoted in Wikipedia, https://en.wikipedia.org/wiki/Warsaw_Uprising

Zuckerman, Marvin (2013), "Why Were the Nazis So Successful at Killing Six Million Jews?", *Jewish Currents*, https://jewishcurrents.org/editor/why-were-the-nazis-so-successful-at-killing-six-million-jews/

Photo Credits

Goldstein Family Photos – 2, 3, 4, 5, 6, 7, 8, 9, 12, 13, 20, 36, 40, 41, 42, 43, 44, 45, 46, 47, 48, 49, 50 many re-photographed by Paul Green and Ron Goldstein

Photos by Norman Miller or Miller collection – 1, 22, 51, 52

Photos by Yad Vashem Archives – cover photos, 21, 23, 24, 25, 28

Photos by Wikimedia Commons – 14, 15, 16, 17, 18, 19, 26, 27, 29, 30, 34, 35, 36, 37

Photos Public Domain – 10, 11, 32

Depositphotos_3417226_xl-2015 (31), Depositphotos_179391904_xl-2015 (33)

Photos by Anastasia Uricher – 38, 39

Select Further Reading List

Dreifuss (Ben Sasson) Havi, (2017) *Relations between Jews and Poles during the Holocaust-The Jewish Perspectives* Jerusalem: Yad Vashem

Grabowski, Jan (2013) *Hunt for the Jews. Betrayal and Murder in German Occupied Poland* Bloomington: Indiana University Press

Gross, Jan T. (2001) *Neighbors: The Destruction of the Jewish Community in Jedwabne, Poland* Princeton University Press

Gunnar S. Paulson (2003) *The Secret City: The Hidden Jews of Warsaw* New Haven: Yale University Press

Harari, Fiona (2018) *We Are Here: Talking with Australia's oldest Holocaust survivors,* Scribe Publications.

Kwiet, Konrad and Matthäus, Jürgen (eds.) (2004) *Contemporary Responses to the Holocaust* Westport, Conn: Praeger

Lawson, Tom & Jordan, James (eds.) (2007) *The Memory of the Holocaust in Australia* London/Portland: Valletine Mitchell

Lipski, Sam and Rutland, Suzanne D. (2015) *Let My People Go: The Untold Story of Australia and the Soviet Jews 1959-89* Hybrid Publishers

Rutland, Suzanne, D. (2016) *The Jews in Australia* Cambridge: Cambridge University Press

Sharon Kangisser Cohen, "Why We Choose Australia" in Ofer, Dalia et.al. (eds.) (2012) *Holocaust Survivors. Resettlement. Memories, Identities.* New York/Oxford: Berghahn Books pp 275-292

Sydney Jewish Museum on Lena Goldstein *Liberation: In Bunkers and Shelters* (SJM 5467)

Sydney Jewish Museum (2017) *Closure. Portraits of Survival* (SJM 2017, 34-35)

Sydney Jewish Museum (2018) Survivor Portraits, Helena (Lena) Goldstein

Books by the Author

Miller, B. (2018) *The Dying Days of Segregation in Australia: Case Study Yarrabah*. Barbara Miller Books.

Miller, B. (2018) *White Woman Black Heart: Journey Home to Old Mapoon, a Memoir*. Createspace.

Miller, B. ed. (2015) author Munganbana Norman Miller *Reef and Rainforest: An Aboriginal Voice Through Art and Story*, Adelaide: Renbro.

Miller, B. (2014) *The European Quest to Find Terra Australis Incognita: Quiros, Torres and Janszoon*, Sydney; Writers and eBooks.

Miller, B. (2012) *William Cooper, Gentle Warrior: Standing Up for Australian Aborigines and Persecuted Jews*, Xlibris.

Miller, B. (2006) "The Re-Founding of Australia" in Maeliau, M., Maki, J., Miller, B. and Siilata, M. *Uluru: The Heart of Australia*, Honiara, Solomon Is.

Miller, B. (1992) "A Social-Historical and Psychological Perspective on Aboriginal Intra-Cultural Aggression" in Thomas, D. and Veno, A. (Eds) *Psychology and Social Change, Creating an International Agenda*, The Dunmore Press: Palmerston North, New Zealand.

Roberts, J.P., Russell, B., and Parsons, M., (1975) (Eds) *The Mapoon Story by The Mapoon People*, Volume 1, International Development Action: Fitzroy, Victoria and printed by Amber Press, Sydney.

Roberts, J.P., Parsons, M., and Russell, B. (1975) *The Mapoon Story According to the Invaders: Church Mission, Queensland Government and Mining Company*, Volume 2, International Development Action: Fitzroy, Victoria and printed by Amber Press, Sydney. (Author's maiden name was Russell)

Free

I'd like to give you a free chapter from another book of mine. It tells you the untold story of the first Europeans to set foot on Australia. It was at Mapoon. Just use this link to download it.

http://eepurl.com/dn69ab

If you enjoyed my book, please go to Amazon and leave a few comments as a review and/or send me a few comments at bmiller-books@bigpond.com

And visit my facebook page - https://www.facebook.com/Barbara-Miller-Books-479991872149265/

Keep a lookout for more books in the Faces of Eve Series

Made in the USA
Coppell, TX
17 December 2020